CAREERS

IN ARCHITECTURE

VGM Professional Careers Series

CAREERS
IN ARCHITECTURE

BLYTHE CAMENSON

WITHDRAWN

VGM Career Books

Chicago   New York   San Francisco   Lisbon   London   Madrid   Mexico City
Milan   New Delhi   San Juan   Seoul   Singapore   Sydney   Toronto

Library of Congress Cataloging-in-Publication Data

Camenson, Blythe.
    Careers in architecture / Blythe Camenson.
        p.   cm. — (VGM professional careers)
    Includes bibliographical references.
    ISBN 0-658-00456-5 (hardcover) — ISBN 0-658-00460-3 (pbk.)
    1. Architecture—Vocational guidance—United States.   I. Title.   II. VGM
professional careers series.

    Arch. NA1995 .C257 ~~2001~~ 2002
      720'.23'73—dc21
                                                    2001026432

VGM Career Books

A Division of The McGraw·Hill Companies

1 2 3 4 5 6 7 8 9 0 LBM/LBM 0 9 8 7 6 5 4 3 2 1

ISBN 0-658-00456-5 (hardcover)
ISBN 0-658-00460-3 (paperback)

This book was set in Times
Printed and bound by Lake Book Manufacturing

Cover photograph copyright © PhotoDisc

McGraw-Hill books are available at special quantity discounts to use as premiums and
sales promotions, or for use in corporate training programs. For more information, please
write to the Director of Special Sales, Professional Publishing, McGraw-Hill, Two Penn
Plaza, New York, NY 10121-2298. Or contact your local bookstore.

This book is printed on acid-free paper.

CONTENTS

ABOUT THE AUTHOR

Blythe Camenson is a full-time writer with more than four dozen books to her credit, most on the subject of various careers. She is also the coauthor of *Your Novel Proposal: From Creation to Contract* (Writer's Digest Books) and director of Fiction Writer's Connection, a membership organization for new writers (www.fictionwriters.com).

ACKNOWLEDGMENTS

The author would like to thank the following professionals for providing information about their careers:

Joel André, architect
Peter Benton, architect
Greg Blackwell, landscape architect/interiorscaper
Kent Brinkley, landscape architect/garden historian
David DiCicco, architect
John Downs, professor
Gary Fischer, architect
George Hallowell, architect
Julie Haney, architect
Jasper (Joe) Hardesty, architect
Steve Lazarian, licensed general contractor
Judy Moore, architect
Harvey Schorr, architect
Lee Sullivan Hill, cost estimator
Maggie Shannon Wagenaar, civil engineer
Matthew Zehnder, landscape architect/regional planner

Part One
Careers in Architecture

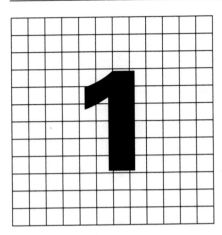

THE FIELD OF ARCHITECTURE

Architecture is the profession of designing buildings, open areas, and even whole communities, often with an eye to the aesthetics of the end result. The word *architecture* also refers to the overall design: the architecture of New Orleans, of Paris, and so on.

Architects are the trained professionals who design buildings and other structures. The design of a building involves far more than just its appearance, however. Buildings must also be functional, safe, and economical, and must suit the needs of the people who use them. The architect who designs a new library and forgets to calculate the weight of the books the floor needs to support is doing his or her client and the community a disservice, and won't be in business for very long. Architects must take every detail into consideration when they design buildings and other structures.

A HISTORY OF ARCHITECTURAL EDUCATION

MIT in Cambridge, Massachusetts, was the first institution to offer formal education in architecture. The year was 1865, some fifty years after Thomas Jefferson, the States' only architect-president, proposed a professional curriculum in architecture be established in the School of Mathematics of the University of Virginia. Because the search for an appropriately trained instructor yielded no one, the program was delayed for many years.

In 1867 the University of Illinois at Urbana and in 1871 Cornell University followed MIT. Canada entered the field of training architects with the Universities of Toronto and Montreal in 1876.

The Morrill Act, passed by Congress in 1862, affected the focus of higher education for architecture, as well as other fields. In exchange for land granted by the U.S. government (thus the term *land-grant colleges*), colleges were directed to provide practical, hands-on education for U.S. students. This approach was in sharp contrast with the European style that more clearly separated education and training. In other words, you were "educated" at the university and, once on the job, you were "trained." Although not all institutions of higher education founded since then are land-grant colleges, the tradition of the system developed was strongly pervasive, particularly in the South, Midwest, and West. In spite of the American land-grant influence, the European tradition also had important historical impact in architectural education in North America.

Many people thought the practical education approach to be uncultured. Looking to Europe for guidance, as Americans often did in the nineteenth century, attention focused on the distinguished Ecole des Beaux Arts in Paris as the epitome of architectural training. The Ecole's philosophy was imported to the United States, and most architecture schools in the early part of this century had at least one Paris-trained professor. Those who were not lucky enough to have a French architect as an instructor could travel to Paris and attend the program for a year directly. Graduate courses in New York were also taught by members of the Beaux Arts staff. Canada was also importing a number of Beaux Arts–trained teachers at this time, but because Canada had a stronger connection with England than did the United States, many of Canada's first instructors came from the British Isles.

The jury system still in place today to judge art shows and other artistic events developed as a result of the Beaux Arts system. Students were assigned a design problem early in the first term, and their progress in solving this problem was carefully watched and encouraged through close supervision. At the end of the time period, drawings were delivered to the "master" for critique. The Beaux Arts system relied heavily on brilliant teachers and learning by doing. Competition was intense, and the end results were beautifully drawn projects in traditional styles that were often workable only on the basis of "good taste" and intuition. The style was mostly neoclassical, and the favorite building type was the monument. These creative projects were judged by a jury of highly regarded professors and guest architects.

In the early part of the twentieth century, both the United States and Canada started developing their own cultures and shying away from European influence. Changes in architecture in Europe, the growing fame of Chicago skyscrapers, and Frank Lloyd Wright's "Prairie School" architecture all contributed to change in North America.

Architectural education started in different ways on different campuses. There are separate and autonomous schools or colleges of architecture; departments and programs within graduate schools; schools of art or design; schools oriented toward engineering, technology, or sociology; and, more recently, schools of urban planning and design. For example, the University of Oregon's architecture program, started in 1914, was the first in the United States to affiliate itself with the allied arts—painting, crafts, and sculpture—rather than with engineering. Columbia University shifted in 1934 away from the French method toward those of the modern German movement highlighted by the Bauhaus school. The Bauhaus, formed in 1919, moved to its famous Dessau, Germany, location in 1925, but was closed down by the Nazis in 1933. The influence of that school was felt throughout the world, however. Instruction was of a practical nature, providing actual work for buildings under construction.

In 1936 Walter Gropius, the Bauhaus' director, came to the United States and was head of the architecture department at Harvard University from 1938 to 1952. In the same year, Harvard joined architecture, landscape architecture, and urban planning into one school, the triangular model for many schools today. Two years later, the famous architect Ludwig Mies van der Rohe—a colleague of Gropius—also came to the United States, and become the head of the architecture school at the Illinois Institute of Technology. In 1922 Cornell University was the first school to adopt a five-year professional program of study in architecture. This became standard practice in all architecture schools by 1940.

Architecture continues to change and increase in complexity. Projects in general are larger, with many new technological developments, such as automatic control systems for air-conditioning, or factory prefabrication. Efficient use of energy and ecologically responsible design have also become important.

Another change is today's client. No longer do architects work only with a private individual. More often than not the client today is a board of directors or trustees, a special committee, or representatives of a government agency.

THE DUTIES OF THE ARCHITECT

While architects generally start their careers from the same jumping-off place— a professional degree in architecture—the paths they take from that point onward can vary immensely. There are many roles an architect can play and many settings to play them in. Architecture is not a profession that will stifle its members.

Architects provide professional services to individuals and organizations planning a construction project. They may be involved in all phases of development, from the initial discussion with the client through the entire construction process. The architect and client discuss the objectives, requirements, and budget of a project. In some cases, architects provide various predesign services—conducting feasibility and environmental impact studies, selecting a site, or specifying the requirements the design must meet. For example, they may determine space requirements by researching the number and type of potential users of a building. The architect then prepares drawings and a report presenting ideas for the client to review.

After the initial proposals are discussed and accepted, architects develop final construction plans. These plans show the building's appearance and details for its construction. Accompanying these are drawings of the structural system; air-conditioning, heating, and ventilating systems; electrical systems; plumbing; and possibly site and landscape plans. Architects also specify the building materials and, in some cases, the interior furnishings. In developing designs, architects follow building codes, zoning laws, fire regulations, and other ordinances, such as those requiring easy access by disabled persons.

Throughout the planning stage, they make necessary changes. Although they have traditionally used pencil and paper to produce design and construction drawings, architects are increasingly turning to computer-aided design and drafting (CADD) technology for these important tasks.

Architects may also assist the client in obtaining construction bids, selecting a contractor, and negotiating the construction contract. As construction proceeds, they may visit the building site to ensure the contractor is following the design, adhering to the schedule, using the specified materials, and meeting quality work standards.

The job is not complete until all construction is finished, required tests are made, and construction costs are paid. Sometimes, architects also provide post-construction services, such as facilities management. They advise on energy efficiency measures, evaluate how well the building design adapts to the needs of occupants, and make necessary improvements.

WORKING CONDITIONS FOR ARCHITECTS

Architects usually work in a comfortable environment. Most of their time is spent in offices consulting with clients, developing reports and drawings, and working with other architects and engineers. However, they often visit construction sites to review the progress of projects. Architects may occasionally be under stress, working nights and weekends to meet deadlines. Almost two out of five architects work more than forty hours a week, in contrast to one in four workers in all other occupations combined.

EMPLOYMENT OPPORTUNITIES

Because of the unusual scope of architecture programs, both public and private sectors offer a wide range of opportunities for architecture degree holders. In addition to traditional practice in private architectural firms, architecture graduates are commonly employed in public and government agencies, community design and urban planning firms, building and construction firms, community development corporations, and building products manufacturers. Alternate career paths may lead into related disciplines discussed later in this chapter.

JOB OUTLOOK FOR ARCHITECTS

Prospective architects may face competition for entry-level jobs, especially if the number of architectural degrees awarded remains at current levels or increases. Employment of architects is projected to grow about as fast as the average for all occupations through 2008, and additional job openings will stem from the need to replace architects who retire or leave the labor force for other reasons. However, many individuals are attracted to this occupation, and the number of applicants often exceeds the number of available jobs, especially in the most prestigious firms. Prospective architects who complete at least one summer internship—either paid or unpaid—while in school and who know CADD technology (especially that which conforms to the new national standards) will have a distinct advantage in obtaining an intern-architect position after graduation.

Employment of architects is strongly tied to the level of local construction, particularly nonresidential structures such as office buildings, shopping centers, schools, and health-care facilities. After a boom in nonresidential construction during the 1980s, building slowed significantly during the first half of the 1990s. Despite slower labor force growth and increases in telecommuting and flexi-place work, however, nonresidential construction is expected to grow more quickly through 2008 than during the previous decade, driving demand for more architects.

As the stock of buildings ages, demand for remodeling and repair work should grow considerably. The needed renovation and rehabilitation of old buildings, particularly in urban areas where space for new buildings is becoming limited, is expected to provide many job opportunities for architects.

In addition, demographic trends and changes in health-care delivery are influencing the demand for certain institutional structures, and should also provide more jobs for architects in the future. Growth is expected in the number of adult care centers, assisted-living facilities, and community health clinics, all of which are preferable, less costly alternatives to hospitals and nursing homes. In addition, increases in the school-age population have resulted in new school construction. Additions to existing schools (especially colleges and universities), as well as overall modernization, will continue to add to demand for architects through 2008.

Because construction—particularly office and retail construction—is sensitive to cyclical changes in the economy, architects will face particularly strong competition for jobs or clients during recessions, and layoffs may occur. Those involved in the design of institutional buildings such as schools, hospitals, nursing homes, and correctional facilities will be less affected by fluctuations in the economy.

Even in times of overall good job opportunities, however, there may be areas of the country with poor opportunities. Architects who are licensed to practice in one state must meet the licensing requirements of other states before practicing elsewhere. These requirements are becoming more standardized, however, facilitating movement between states.

TYPES OF ARCHITECTURAL OFFICES

Architectural practices are usually structured on one of two basic models. The first consists of a series of departmental specializations: designers, specification writers, structural experts, landscape designers, production draftsmen, and so on. A project starts in one division and is passed to the next as work progresses. In such instances very few people will see the job all the way through to completion, but each performs a specific function for each job the office undertakes.

The other model divides the office into teams, with each team responsible for its own projects from start to finish. There may be various specialists on the team or consultants may be used. A team may be working on several jobs simultaneously, but will have little, if any, responsibility for other projects being undertaken by other teams.

Few offices precisely fit these simplified models, and many have certain aspects of both. Some architectural firms subcontract with consultants and other firms for major portions of the project, thus keeping their own staff to a minimal number. In fact, principals of large firms may spend little of their time on actual design or drawings for new buildings. Architects working in large firms are not solely responsible for a complete building. A large and complex building, such as a $100-million hospital, may require three to four years from preliminary programming to completion, with as many as forty people working nearly full-time on this one project.

Depending on the particular model a firm follows, the roles for architects may range from design to management, or anywhere in-between. While larger firms may offer opportunities to specialize in a particular aspect of the practice, smaller firms often require the architect to master many different facets of the profession. Common practice roles include project management, facilities planning, site planning and design, technical research and specifications, document production, contract administration, urban design and planning, interior design, and practice management.

GETTING THAT FIRST JOB

New graduates usually begin as intern-architects in architectural firms, where they assist in preparing architectural documents or drawings. They may also do research on building codes and materials, or write specifications for building materials, installation criteria, the quality of finishes, and other related details. Internship for those graduates working toward an ultimate goal of licensure to practice architecture is intended as a continuation of the process of architectural education, providing specialized training and knowledge about architectural practice that is not usually covered in the academic setting.

New graduates often seek a private architecture firm as the setting for their first job. For interns, diversified experience under the supervision of a registered architect in such a firm is the fastest and most typical way to fulfill the training requirements for registration. But, because most firms are small, interns don't often see the first place of employment as the ultimate one. Rather, this is a chance to learn and contribute, develop the everyday skills of practice, and better understand just where each intern's place may be within the profession and the building enterprise.

An internship is a two-way street, though. The employer expects the intern to bring to the job basic professional skills, to use those skills in performing professional services, and to learn how the firm practices architecture. As in any employment setting, the goals of intern and firm may not overlap completely; the secret to a successful internship lies in exploiting and expanding the area of overlap as quickly and as effectively as possible.

Some firms take a strong interest in the growth of their interns, pointing toward registration as an architect and expanded responsibilities leading to those of the project architect. These firms may be active in the Intern Development Program (IDP) (see Chapter 2 for more information) and aim to provide specific opportunities for the growth and development of their interns. For most firms, however, the process is less structured. To meet the demands of projects and clients within tight economic constraints, a firm is not left with much time or money for intern development.

For interns, professional development is important. When choosing the first position, the American Institute of Architects (AIA) suggests you use this list of questions as a guide:

- What is the firm's basic attitude toward interns? Am I there to "fill a slot," or is the firm interested in my professional growth?

- What are my long-term prospects for remaining with the firm? Do interns tend to move on after they are licensed, or do they remain?

- Does the firm invest in the professional growth of its interns?

- Will there be opportunities to participate in education programs for interns? Will there be time to prepare for the registration exam?

- Will I have a mentor?

- Does the firm participate in the Intern Development Program?

The answers to these questions don't all have to be yes. Interns consider many factors in selecting a firm. If they are on the path to registration, though, personal growth and diversity of experience are important. For further investigation, look at the firms in the region(s) you are considering. Construction Market Data's *Profile* is a good place to start; it provides contacts, telephone numbers, and enough information about a practice to help you qualify—or disqualify— some firms. Your local AIA chapter office may publish classified listings or maintain a file of job opportunities in your area. Also check the AIA website for current job listings (www.aiaonline.com).

There are many other valuable sources of information for job opportunities in this field, including your local architecture school. Many employers post job listings in college and university architecture departments—even for experienced people. Some schools also maintain placement services for finishing students and alumni. You should never underestimate the power of word of mouth and networking, so keep in touch with classmates. Most schools maintain current addresses of alumni; you may want to scan these for contacts in firms or other practice settings that interest you. Finally, look around at what's being proposed and built. Who's doing work that interests you? These would be people to contact.

STARTING YOUR OWN FIRM

Once the architect has fulfilled internship requirements and is registered, opportunities for firm ownership are a real possibility. Reasons to move into self-employment can vary: perhaps partnership in the current employer's firm doesn't seem likely, or philosophies clash or differ. As a profession of small (and often closely held) firms, the goal of ownership is most frequently achieved by starting up a firm, whether as a sole proprietor or in collaboration with one or two others with common goals and ideally with complementary skills. About a thousand new firms start up each year.

SAMPLE INTERN JOB OPENINGS

These listings are provided as a sample only and as such, the hiring firms are not mentioned. You can locate similar listings by searching the Internet using keywords such as "architecture," "jobs," "careers," and so on.

Intern, Georgia

An international firm located in Atlanta is seeking an intern-architect to work on commercial projects including aviation, military, industrial, sports, and criminal justice facilities. Qualified candidate will have architectural degree or background (NAAB-accredited professional degree preferred), approximately zero to three years' experience, CADD literate (Microstation preferred) with good graphic capabilities and verbal communication skills. Competitive salary and benefit package.

Intern, Mississippi

Small firm focusing in historic preservation, new construction within the context of historic buildings and innovative residential projects seeks enthusiastic intern-architect with a desire to work and live in a great small town in Mississippi. Individual will bring fresh, creative ideas to work on award-winning projects. Bachelor's degree in architecture, AutoCAD proficient, and a keen desire to advance your skills. Excellent working environment and comprehensive benefits.

Intern, Texas

Large Texas firm has full-time position available for an intermediate architect or intern with two to six years' experience in commercial architecture. We prefer a candidate with strong design and production skills who is seeking a ground-level opportunity with a growing architectural practice. The position offers long-term commitment and career advancement for the right individual. Staff members are offered the option of a traditional office workplace or working from a remote home office with flexible hours. The successful candidate will be a responsible, self-motivated, proactive individual who enjoys a degree of autonomy in the workplace. Experience with ArchiCAD is a plus.

EARNINGS FOR ARCHITECTS

Architecture, in general, is not a career that brings much fame and fortune. Only a few architects have become household names through the ages. Architectural employees may be paid either an hourly wage or annual salary. According to the American Institute of Architects, the median compensation, including bonuses, for intern-architects in architectural firms was $35,200 in 1999. Licensed architects with three to five years' experience had median earnings of $41,100; licensed architects with eight to ten years of experience, but who were not managers or principals of a firm, earned $54,700. These salaries are much less than for the related engineering fields. (See Chapter 7.) Principals or partners of firms had median earnings of $132,500 in 1999, although partners in some large practices earned considerably more. Similar to other industries, small architectural firms (fewer than five employees) are less likely than larger firms to provide employee benefits, although some firms have profit-sharing plans for those who are not partners.

Earnings of partners in established architectural firms may fluctuate because of changing business conditions. Some architects may have difficulty establishing their own practices, and may go through a period when their expenses are greater than their income, requiring substantial financial resources.

RELATED FIELDS

Architects—and sometimes interns on their way to registration—soon discover there are many settings in which to develop their skills and interests. Some seek community design and urban planning firms (see Chapter 8), public agencies, and private community development corporations. Others find the construction environment more to their taste, finding positions with contractors, developers, and building products manufacturers or suppliers (see Chapter 9). Still others discover they can manage and design projects within corporate, institutional, and governmental facilities offices.

Some career paths lead out of architecture practice and into related activities, such as architectural history, historic preservation (Chapter 4), or computer-aided design, or allied disciplines, including planning, landscape architecture (Chapter 6), engineering (Chapter 7), or interior design, or related industries, such as computer software development, real estate, finance, or law. Teaching and research provide yet another practice setting for many architecture graduates (Chapter 5). Some of these alternate career paths do not require architectural licensure, but may necessitate additional education, training, or certification required by the particular allied profession.

What follows is a bird's-eye look at some related fields. Other alternative and related fields are covered in subsequent chapters.

Interior design. Interior design requires expertise in areas such as space planning, finish materials, acoustics, lighting, selection and purchase of furnishings and furniture, and ergonomic and behavioral sciences—that is, the nonstructural aspects of building interiors. Specialties have emerged in the interior design of commercial offices, stage sets, retail stores, hotels, restaurants, historic styles and preservation, ship and aircraft interiors, and furniture design. Across the country, there are undergraduate and graduate programs in interior architecture and interior design, and some states license or certify interior designers.

Lighting design. The lighting designer's challenge is to illuminate with purpose, providing visual comfort, efficiency, productivity, and, in some cases, drama. Successful lighting designers combine an aesthetic sense of color and form, a solid grasp of the technology of light (lamps, fixtures, controls, and accessories), and an ability to integrate natural and artificial lighting in architecture. Many of today's practicing lighting designers are trained as interior or industrial designers or as electrical engineers, although architecture schools are becoming important participants in lighting education and research.

Acoustical design. The demand for proper acoustics is inherent in all building types. Good acoustics are as important for comfort and productivity in homes, offices, schools, and shopping centers as they are in churches and concert halls. Increasingly, acousticians also must know how to work with the electronic systems that control or enhance existing sound in space—or even "shape" space for listening. Educated as engineers, physicists, and occasionally architects, acousticians usually work as independent consultants in small firms.

Environmental and behavioral research. In their pursuit of foundations in research for design and building, some architects move in behavioral directions, doing advanced study in environmental design, psychology, or sociology. These individuals often seek teaching and research appointments. Some form consultancies offering postoccupancy evaluations and participating in the facilities-management process.

FIRSTHAND ACCOUNTS

What better way to learn about a field than to hear from those personally involved in it? Included throughout this book are firsthand accounts from a range of architects—residential, commercial, historic preservation, and landscape—and engineers and planners. You will note throughout these accounts that many architects work for firms that choose not to specialize in only one area of architecture, and that they keep specialists on staff in a variety of areas. This keeps firms much more competitive with others in the marketplace. Read what they have to say about getting started and what the work is like, including the upsides and downsides, then make your own conclusions.

Choosing a career in architecture can lead you in a number of different directions. The more informed you are, the more informed your choices can be, and the more ultimately satisfying your career will be.

PREPARING FOR A CAREER IN ARCHITECTURE

As of January 1999 in the United States, to call yourself an architect you must have a license that is issued by a state, the District of Columbia, or a U.S. territory. Architecture school graduates may work in the field before they are licensed, but a licensed architect is required to take legal responsibility for all work. Licensing requirements include a professional degree in architecture, a period of practical training or internship, and passage of all sections of the Architect Registration Examination (ARE).

The National Architectural Accrediting Board (NAAB), established in 1940, is the sole agency authorized to accredit U.S. professional degrees in architecture. Since most state registration boards in the United States require any applicant for licensure to have graduated from an NAAB-accredited program, obtaining such a degree is an essential aspect of preparing for the professional practice of architecture. However, state architectural registration boards set their own standards, so graduation from a non–NAAB-accredited program may meet the educational requirement for licensing in some states. There are currently 123 schools in the United States and 10 in Canada offering professional programs in architecture, leading to the Bachelor of Architecture or Master of Architecture degree. (For a full list see Appendix C.)

TYPES OF DEGREES

Several types of professional degrees in architecture are available through colleges and universities. The majority of all architectural degrees are from five-year Bachelor of Architecture programs, intended for students entering from high school or with no previous architectural training. Some schools offer a two-year Master of Architecture program for students with a preprofessional undergraduate degree in architecture or a related area, or a three- or four-year Master of Architecture program for students with a degree in another discipline. In addition, there are many combinations and variations of these programs.

The choice of degree type depends upon each individual's preference and educational background. Prospective architecture students should consider the available options before committing to a program. For example, although the five-year Bachelor of Architecture program offers the fastest route to the professional degree, courses are specialized and, if the student does not complete the program, moving to a nonarchitectural program may be difficult.

All degrees outside of the field of architecture are referred to as *nonarchitecture degrees*. This title generally describes degrees in fields such as philosophy, biology, engineering, and also undesignated bachelor of arts and bachelor of science degrees. These undesignated B.A. or B.S. degrees often provide opportunities for a major or minor in architectural studies or environmental design offered through a liberal studies program. The proportion of architectural studies in the B.A. or B.S. major usually does not exceed 50 percent of the four-year program and may or may not provide for advanced standing in a professional architecture degree program. Architecture degrees fit into one of the four following categories: preprofessional architecture degrees, professional architecture degrees, post-professional architecture degrees, and nonprofessional graduate architecture degrees.

Preprofessional Architecture Degree

This term refers to architecturally focused four-year degrees that are not professional degrees (and thus cannot be accredited). These degrees have such titles as B.S. in Architecture, B.S. in Architectural Studies, B.A. in Architecture, Bachelor of Environmental Design, Bachelor of Architectural Studies, etc.; the amount of architecture work in the program varies and will determine the length of time required to complete further professional architecture studies.

Professional Architecture Degree

A professional architecture degree is one that may be accredited by NAAB or CACB. Accredited degrees are required by most jurisdictions for licensure as an architect. These degrees are either the Bachelor of Architecture (B.Arch.) degree or the Master of Architecture (M.Arch.) degree. The Bachelor of Architecture normally requires at least five years to complete. The Master of Architecture requires from one to five years to complete depending on the individual student's previous education. When the master's degree follows a four-year, preprofessional architecture degree, it represents the "two" in the term *four-plus-two program*, and is the final portion of the professional phase of the study program.

Post-Professional Architecture Degree

This is a graduate degree offered to students who already have a professional degree in architecture. Such degree programs are not accredited by NAAB and CACB. The degrees may be in highly specialized areas of study such as design theory, health-care facilities, preservation, interior design, solar design, and so on. This type of degree can be either a master's degree or, in a few cases, a Ph.D. or other doctorate.

Nonprofessional Graduate Architecture Degree

This title refers to graduate degrees in architecture offered to students who do not have a professional degree and wish to pursue nonprofessional graduate work in architecture. These programs vary widely in duration and degree title.

PATHS TO THE PROFESSIONAL DEGREE

There are three usual paths to obtaining the professional degree in architecture:

1. Obtaining a Bachelor of Architecture degree;

2. Obtaining a preprofessional degree plus a professional Master of Architecture degree (the program commonly referred to as the "four-plus-two" route falls in this category); or

3. Obtaining a four-year nonarchitecture degree plus a three- to four-year professional Master of Architecture degree.

The majority of students enter architecture through the first two routes; however, the third route is also viable. An explanation of each follows.

Path 1: Bachelor of Architecture Degree

The professional Bachelor of Architecture degree is often the most expeditious means of obtaining the professional degree required for licensure. This route normally requires a minimum of five years of study followed by a three-year internship.

Although a five-year program provides the quickest route to satisfy the academic requirements for licensure, speed is not necessarily synonymous with what may be best for every individual. Many Bachelor of Architecture programs begin with a concentration of architecture courses in a fairly prescribed manner, although some schools begin with a general course of instruction. Electives tend to be few and exposure to other fields limited. As a result, the approximately 50 percent of entering students who do not complete the program may have difficulty moving into another area without some loss of credit.

Many Bachelor of Architecture programs, however, have devised curriculum structures that allow for quite a bit of flexibility. These programs are broken into yearly components separating the general instruction and preprofessional requirements from the concentration of architecture courses that follows of two plus three, one plus four, three plus two, or four plus one year. The breaks between the components of the program indicate logical entry and exit points from the various phases of the full five-year program.

In most schools the student's work is carefully reviewed before advancement to the next phase. Such points provide a relatively easy means of transfer into an architecture program; transfer to another institution, particularly between degrees; or transfer to another academic discipline. The logical break points may also be used by the faculty to transfer out students who have demonstrated little progress. The early segments of the curriculum mix preprofessional design courses with liberal arts and often serve as a common base for several different environmental design disciplines such as architecture, landscape architecture, industrial design, or graphic design.

Most professional degree programs also accept transfer students at the designated break points, but transfer credit is usually evaluated on an individual course-by-course and case-by-case basis. While the structure of some programs makes it relatively easy for a professional school to accept transfer students from both junior colleges and other colleges, it is recommended in most instances that a student considering an architecture degree start either at the professional school or at a school with a preprofessional program.

Path 2: Preprofessional Bachelor's Plus Master of Architecture

The preprofessional degree plus professional Master of Architecture degree is the other predominant route to obtaining a professional architecture degree. This route normally requires six years to complete, followed by a three-year internship. The flexibility in the program is readily apparent. At the end of four years the student has a college degree and may decide to continue in architecture and get the professional master's degree, spend a year or two working for an architect, or change disciplines and pursue study in another design-related field. Or the graduate may decide at this point to shift careers completely and/or seek an advanced degree outside the design field.

Preprofessional programs are not professionally accredited and vary widely with respect to title, emphasis, electives, requirements, and specific architecture offerings. They are, however, preparatory for advanced architectural or other environmental design fields. The four-year preprofessional program may be subdivided into two phases, usually of two years each. The pre-architecture program may have only basic introductory courses in architecture with the majority of the course work focusing on the arts, humanities, and sciences. The typical program, like the subdivided five-year professional programs, is highly flexible and provides a general education in the early years. While this may frustrate many who want to immerse themselves quickly in architecture, it does provide time for experiencing a wider range of subjects, allowing the maturing student a better opportunity to make career choices. Ideally, the extra courses in the humanities and social sciences will give students a broader background from which to start their professional education. For those who ultimately receive advanced degrees in design areas other than architecture—or in nonarchitecture subjects (such as business or structural engineering)—the four-year degree may be preferable to the five-year professional program in minimizing course work and time. One other advantage of a four-plus-two program is the potential for earning the professional degree at an institution other than where the undergraduate work was completed.

The graduate degree component of the four-plus-two path is the professional NAAB- or CACB-accredited (for Canada) degree. This degree is most appropriate for students who have a four-year preprofessional undergraduate degree in architecture. The course of study generally takes two years; however, at some schools, up to three years is required. These programs are designed to provide the professional education of the student as well as provide an opportunity for independent and creative exploration. It is imperative that the master's degree program be accredited if the student wishes to obtain the professional degree and licensure.

In addition to the standard four-plus-two path, the NAAB has recently recognized a five-and-a-half-year Master of Architecture program, which may be entered directly from high school. In this case, students enroll in a program that may lead directly to a Master of Architecture degree, following a curriculum that is similar to that of a Bachelor of Architecture program. Students must be expressly accepted into the university's graduate school to pursue the final phase of this degree. Those who do not qualify for graduate study have the option of completing a nonprofessional undergraduate degree, with the possibility of pursuing the master's degree in one of the more traditional paths at another institution.

Several schools are now considering converting their B.Arch. programs over the coming years to M.Arch. programs, either along the lines described above or by offering a bachelor's degree and an M.Arch. simultaneously at the end of a five- or five-and-a-half-year period of study.

Path 3: Nonarchitecture Bachelor's Plus Master of Architecture

The nonarchitecture degree plus professional master's degree path is the third route available, but is the least traveled option. This route normally requires seven-and-a-half years of study (a four-year undergraduate degree plus a three-and-a-half-year Master of Architecture degree), followed by a three-year internship. This route is usually taken by those who have embarked on a career other than architecture and later decide to study architecture. Many people enter the profession this way; their average age is in the late twenties and their undergraduate backgrounds range across every imaginable discipline. Students entering the profession this way are usually quite mature and serious about their studies. This course of study requires three to four years beyond the undergraduate degree. The immersion into architecture is quick and very intense. Some schools provide all of the education at the graduate level, while others will admit degree holders into their professional master's program with "deficiencies." This means that preparatory undergraduate course work must first be successfully completed before formal admittance to the graduate program. Like the two-year Master of Architecture degree, however, the three-and-a-half year M.Arch. may be a fully NAAB- or CACB-accredited professional degree program, and successful graduates have professional education credentials equal to those with a B.Arch. or other M.Arch.

COURSE OF STUDY

A typical program includes courses in architectural history and theory, building design, professional practice, math, physical sciences, and liberal arts.

Central to most architectural programs is the design studio, where students put into practice the skills and concepts learned in the classroom. During the final semester of many programs, students devote their studio time to creating an architectural project from beginning to end, culminating in a three-dimensional model of their design.

Most architecture graduates do not become principal designers in architectural firms, and there is some criticism that too much emphasis is placed on the design studio without enough attention given to technical instruction. Others argue that the role of the architecture school is not to develop technical skills; rather, it is to provide a broad framework of knowledge and a basic understanding of the desired objectives—realizing that five or six years of formal education cannot possibly provide all the necessary training an architect will ultimately need. But nearly everyone working on an architectural project will at some point be required to make a decision about what materials should be used or how they will be applied. Literally thousands of details must be resolved before the building is completed. To this extent everyone is a "designer," and this in part explains the emphasis on design in architecture schools.

A typical architecture program will recognize the importance of graphic skills, and early instruction will be given in freehand drawing and graphic delineation. Various media will be explored, including pencil, ink, color, and often computer graphics. The problem of designing a structure to withstand the forces of gravity, wind, and earthquakes is usually addressed through a series of courses. Beginning with algebra, trigonometry, and physics, most schools require at least one course in calculus and descriptive geometry before the introduction of engineering statics (a development of the study of vector forces from elementary physics). There may be an additional course on structural materials, particularly in engineering-oriented programs. The actual structures courses may be organized by the structural element—beam, column, and so on—or the structural material—wood, steel, reinforced concrete.

Many schools of architecture also offer graduate education for those who already have a bachelor's or master's degree in architecture or other areas. Although graduate education beyond the professional degree is not required for practicing architects, it is for research, teaching, and certain specialties.

SPECIALIZATION

Specialists exist for nearly every aspect of professional practice: programming, specifications, contracts, cost estimating, construction supervision, site planning, interiors, acoustics, lighting, heating and air-conditioning, and electrical and structural design. If you look through the offerings in the catalogs of several academic programs you will probably find courses covering each of these and other subjects. They may be either required or optional, or may be integrated into a broader course such as Architectural Technology, Professional Practice, Contract Documents, or Building Systems.

THE PORTFOLIO

Most schools of architecture require a portfolio review as part of the admissions process, whether you are applying directly from high school, from within an undergraduate program, or as a returning graduate student. In all these instances, the strongest portfolios tend to be those that demonstrate the creative potential of the candidate, emphasizing the unique strengths and/or talents that the prospective student can bring to the school's program. Whether your talents lie in graphics, design, photography, painting, writing, or any other discipline, approach your portfolio as a design problem, creating a presentation that best showcases your creativity in a clear and professional manner.

SELECTING A SCHOOL

As mentioned earlier, there are more than 130 accredited schools in North America. It's time to narrow your choices. Your first step should be to obtain a copy of the ACSA publication *Guide to Architecture Schools*. The *Guide* is available in most architecture libraries and bookstores, and can also be ordered directly from ACSA. (See Appendix B for ordering information.) The *Guide* outlines each school's program, explaining the basic administrative structure, costs, and enrollment requirements. The listings for ACSA full and candidate member schools describe opportunities and resources available to students, special activities, financial aid, educational philosophy, and programs of study. Choose six or so likely possibilities based on course of study, the geographic region, and whatever other criteria you have set up for your future study. Write or E-mail each one for their college catalogs and other information they might provide. When writing for the college catalogs also ask if there are special brochures prepared by the department or school of architecture. You should read these thoroughly before visiting a school.

Talk to other architects about the schools they went to, or the schools they'd recommend. Practicing architects are busy, but usually quite willing to talk to students.

If possible, arrange to visit the schools that interest you. Plan to come when classes are in session so you can talk to a variety of students at different levels of study. Walk around the campus and the school of architecture. Get a feel for the environment and if this would be the kind of place you'd be willing to spend five or six years of your life.

In choosing your program, remember that some mid-list universities may house excellent schools of architecture, while the famous universities might be the home to only average architecture departments. Of course, make sure the school you choose is accredited by the National Architectural Accrediting Board (NAAB) or the Canadian Architectural Certification Board (CACB). Make sure that the degree you will receive is an accredited professional degree that will fulfill the educational requirement to be eligible for registration. And make sure that course offerings will allow you to focus on any particular interest of yours such as design, computers, energy, sustainability, or preservation, for example.

The amount of financial aid available will play a role, too. Find out if scholarships are available and if they are offered based on academic achievement or on need.

It is impossible to rank architecture schools, so to ask which is the "best" school would not give you a satisfying answer. Best is best for you. The size, location, cost of living, financial aid, programs offered, and so on all add up to suit you or not. No school can be excellent in all aspects. In all likelihood, the most important factor in any educational endeavor is your motivation. Most architectural employers are far more interested in what you have accomplished and will continue to accomplish than in the prestige of your degree.

FINANCING YOUR EDUCATION

Cost should not be an automatic deterrent in deciding the program or the number of years you will study, because most schools are able to offer financial aid. Although some students may find it financially necessary to begin their college education at a community or junior college, for students who are sure that architecture is to be their chosen career field, the five-year professional degree programs offer excellent opportunities. Students seeking slightly more flexibility should also examine five-year programs offering logical curriculum decision points.

Graduate students may receive teaching or research assistantships. You should contact each school you are considering about its current tuition and fees, as well as its potential for providing assistance.

The American Institute of Architects has minimal scholarship programs applicable to schools in the United States, and local AIA chapters may also have scholarships available.

SAMPLE PROGRAMS

The following two programs are chosen only as a sampling to illustrate what is available—their inclusion here is not intended to be an endorsement, nor is the exclusion of other schools intended to show disapproval.

Pratt Institute
School of Architecture
Brooklyn, New York

Bachelor of Architecture   The Bachelor of Architecture program is an accredited program requiring a minimum of five years of study. The 175 credits required for the Bachelor of Architecture degree are organized in three main categories: a core of required courses in architectural study, liberal arts courses, and electives. The core of ninety-eight credits is primarily taken in the first three years and is designed to give basic professional preparation in architectural design, construction, technology, graphic communication, and the humanistic aspects of design.

The liberal arts area requires forty-five credits, of which nine credits are taken within the School of Architecture (Architecture 206, Architecture 207, Architecture 308), six credits in English, six credits in cultural history, six credits in science, and six credits in social science. The remaining twelve credits are taken as electives from among the liberal arts courses offered by the School of Liberal Arts and Sciences.

The elective courses are composed of eighteen credits of professional electives selected from courses offered by the School of Architecture's undergraduate and graduate programs, and fourteen all-Institute electives, which may be selected from courses offered by any school in the Institute. By purposefully selecting courses within all elective areas during their later semesters, students can develop their own unique architectural education in accord with their own needs and goals. Individual curricula may be developed to place more emphasis on such subject areas as advocacy planning, building technology, history and theory, planning, construction management, and urban design.

The degree project year completes the student's academic architectural experience with an in-depth design study, preceded and accompanied by research. The degree project is executed with critics of the student's choice.

Options combining the undergraduate degree with various master's degrees are also available in architecture, planning, and urban design. For more information visit www.pratt.edu/arch/index.html.

University of Manitoba
Department of Architecture
Winnipeg, Manitoba, Canada

**Architecture and
City Planning**   The program combines academic and technical studies to provide students with an understanding of the technology used in the making of built human environment, knowledge and understanding of the interrelationships between natural and the built environments, an understanding of human factors as they shape the design and construction of built environments, and an ability to use visual information and graphic communications and understand spatial analysis in constructing human environments.

The curriculum is structured around four study areas:

1. a central core of design, design theory, and graphics

2. cultural and environmental history

3. building technology and environmental controls

4. plus electives in the humanities, social sciences, and the natural sciences

The design core provides opportunities for students to demonstrate comprehension of knowledge and skills acquired in all four study areas. Students spend twelve contact hours a week in design studios, resolving problems that vary in context from the analysis of a simple natural object, to community spaces, and complex urban problems. Students select an area of specialization such as the Architecture, Landscape Architecture, or City Planning option in their final year, which qualifies them for application to those graduate programs. The program is one of the more demanding undergraduate courses of study at the University of Manitoba, both in terms of contact hours and the time required for completing design and other assignments outside class hours. Consequently, good work habits and a mature and responsible personality are definite assets; particularly, students must learn to budget time so that other course work requirements are not neglected.

The department sets exacting standards for attendance and academic design performance. Its graduates are highly rated among both practicing professionals in architecture, city planning, and landscape architecture, as well as other professional design academic programs of study in North America. The B.E.D. program within the Faculty of Architecture is not specifically concerned with pollution, ecology, biological, or chemical environmental problems. If your interests are in these areas, Environmental Science in the Faculty of Science would be more appropriate.

STUDENT STATISTICS

According to the AIA, 15,312 students were enrolled in full-time B.Arch. accredited programs and 1,606 students were enrolled part-time across the United States in 1999. Full-time M.Arch. candidates totaled 5,769, and there were 689 part-time students. Of these totals, women numbered 4,495; there were 641 African-American students, 78 Native American students, 1,042 Asian/Pacific Isle students, and 929 Hispanic students.

SKILLS AN ARCHITECT MUST HAVE

Architects must be able to visually communicate their ideas to clients. Artistic and drawing ability is very helpful in doing this, but not essential. More important are a visual orientation and the ability to conceptualize and understand spatial relationships. Good verbal and written communication skills, the ability to work independently or as part of a team, and creativity are important qualities for anyone interested in becoming an architect. Computer literacy is also required as most firms use computers for writing specifications, two- and three-dimensional drafting, and financial management. A knowledge of computer-aided design and drafting (CADD) is helpful and will become essential as architectural firms continue to adopt this technology. Recently, the profession recognized National CAD Standards (NCS); architecture students who master NCS will have an advantage in the job market.

TRAINING PERIODS

All state architectural registration boards require a training period before candidates may sit for the ARE and become licensed. Many states have adopted the training standards established by the Intern Development Program (IDP), a branch of the American Institute of Architects and the National Council of Architectural Registration Boards. These standards stipulate broad and diversified training under the supervision of a licensed architect over a three-year period. (Additional information on the IDP is provided later in this chapter.) Graduates with degrees in architecture also enter related fields such as graphic, interior, or industrial design; urban planning; real estate development; civil engineering; or construction management. In such cases an architectural license (and thus the internship period) is not required.

During a training period leading up to licensing as architects, entry-level workers are called *intern-architects*. This training period, which generally lasts three years, allows for practical work experience and a paycheck, while preparing for the Architect Registration Examination (ARE). Typical intern duties may include preparing construction drawings on CADD or assisting in the design of one part of a project.

THE ARE

After completing the internship period, intern-architects are eligible to sit for the ARE. The examination tests candidates on architectural knowledge and is given in sections throughout the year. Candidates who pass the ARE and meet all standards established by their state board are licensed to practice in that state. After becoming licensed and gaining experience, architects take on increasingly responsible duties, eventually managing entire projects. In large firms, architects may advance to supervisory or managerial positions. Some architects become partners in established firms; others set up their own practice.

Several states require continuing education to maintain a license, and many more states are expected to adopt mandatory continuing education. Requirements vary by state, but usually involve the completion of a certain number of credits every year or two through seminars, workshops, formal university classes, conferences, self-study courses, or other sources.

PREPARING EARLY

If you're still in high school while investigating this career, you can prepare by giving yourself a solid background in the physical sciences, including mathematics. You should also be able to conceptualize at an above-average level, have a strong proficiency in oral and written communication, demonstrate a wide interest in the humanities, and be able to draw and sketch with ease. It is doubtful any high school student would be able to master all skill areas, but even a few skills makes a good start. Drawing is probably the most easily acquired skill—math sometimes the most difficult. A good course in freehand drawing would ultimately prove more valuable than drafting; one semester of drafting is probably enough.

Most architecture programs assume entering students have had at least trigonometry and one physics course in high school. Surprisingly, the majority of professional architects are not highly proficient in mathematical skills, and those who are (and hence are strong in structural design) often possess a lower than average ability in drawing or design skills.

Architecture is a highly diversified, multifaceted profession, and the opportunities for specialization are many. So even if you do not excel in math (or drawing or writing), you may still become an outstanding architect. If you spot a weakness in your preparation, do not worry unnecessarily, but do not neglect it as unimportant, either. Overall the architecture school is probably more interested in your class rank, national test scores, and general aptitude than specific courses or skills.

High School Courses to Take

Geography, English, drawing, history, philosophy, and government are useful to everyone. Botany is highly recommended for those planning to pursue landscape architecture. Foreign languages are not often required in architecture programs, but most will accept a language as an elective. With opportunities for study abroad, the right language can have considerable practical use even before graduation, and ease with other languages can also be valuable in the study of architectural history and the conduct of research. For those working for firms with international contacts and contracts, another language would be a plus. A course in industrial arts can be helpful. Speech or debate classes are also important. Architects and architecture students must often express or explain complex ideas orally.

In general, architecture schools expect their students to have above-average intelligence. They want you to be eager to learn and self-motivated and self-disciplined with a broad range of interests.

Summer Work Experience During High School

A summer job in building construction is always useful and sometimes easier to find than a job in a professional architectural firm. If no related jobs are available, make the public library your second home, and study books and magazines on architecture as much as possible. A common deficiency of many architecture students who perform below the average is a lack of interest in reading. Try to address that before starting your professional degree.

Architecture Schools: Special Programs

To provide additional insight into the typical course of study in architecture, many institutions have programs for high school students interested in architectural studies. These programs, usually lasting for several weeks, are designed to be microcosms of the way you will study architecture within a university curriculum. Going through one of these programs may help dispel misconceptions about what architects do and how they learn to do it. ACSA annually publishes a list of summer programs as part of a publication titled *Architecture Schools: Special Programs*. (See Appendix B for more information.)

INTERN DEVELOPMENT PROGRAM

The Intern Development Program (IDP) is a joint program of the American Institute of Architects (AIA), National Council of Architectural Registration Boards (NCARB), and Association of Collegiate Schools of Architecture (ACSA). Currently, all states except California, Missouri, and Arizona require IDP training for initial registration.

The Intern Development Program (IDP) addresses the participant's professional development needs by providing a wide range of resources. The IDP Training Requirement establishes levels of experience in important areas of architectural practice. Through the IDP mentorship system, you receive advice and guidance from practitioners. The IDP record-keeping system facilitates the documentation of internship activities, while the IDP supplementary education system provides a variety of learning resources designed to enrich training.

Many of those who participated in the IDP found that they performed significantly better on the ARE, received relevant and comprehensive preparation for the profession, and developed skills and competencies that are valuable to a firm. In addition, students gained credit for nontraditional work—this is a great way to explore careers in architecture and became eligible for a possible deferment of NDSL and GSL educational loans.

As a student participating in IDP, you may benefit from the informed counsel of experienced practitioners. You may apply work experience toward registration board training requirements after the third year in a B.Arch. or four-plus-two M.Arch. program, and after the first year in a three- or four-year M.Arch. program. You can document your progress through an IDP Council Record. This provides for periodic review of your progress, reduces the time and paperwork needed to apply for registration, becomes part of your portfolio, and documents your versatility to prospective employers. You can plan your work experience using the IDP Core Competencies to map out the skills and knowledge you need to establish yourself as a competent practitioner.

To get involved, contact your school's IDP educator coordinator (usually one of the professional practice faculty), or call AIA at (202) 626-7325 and request IDP Guidelines and an application for an NCARB Council Record. Contact your state registration board and request a copy of the registration requirements.

Apply for your NCARB Council Record. Students and recent graduates (up to six months from graduation) can apply for $50 instead of paying the full fee. The balance of the fee is deferred until you are eligible to take the Architect Registration Examination (ARE).

Contact a local intern who is involved in IDP to establish a mentor relationship while you're still in school. He or she can advise you on how to get the most from your internship, portfolio presentation, job-finding skills and techniques, and firms and wages.

Attend job fairs, firm presentations, and career development lectures sponsored by your AIA chapters. This will help you to learn more about local firms so that you can target the ones you think you'd like. Establish a time line for when you want to become licensed. This will help you establish goals and deadlines.

Review the quality of your internship. If your firm does not have an annual review system, ask your employer and coworkers to evaluate your progress.

Discuss your goals and IDP training expectations for the upcoming year with your mentor. Evaluate how your present firm is helping to achieve your personal and professional goals.

Contact your state registration board to learn about the registration requirements. Verify the ARE application process and deadlines. Review IDP Guidelines and compare the IDP requirements with your state's registration requirements. Contact NCARB and your state registration board to clarify your questions and concerns.

Keep your portfolio up to date. Maintain a daily log of training units in conjunction with your time sheet. Review the IDP core competencies and split up your hours worked into the proper training areas to help expedite your IDP training reports.

Talk with other interns. Find out about their firms' projects and share your internship experiences.

IDP CORE COMPETENCIES

AIA, in conjunction with NCARB, has identified the core competencies that are necessary to adequately measure the ability of an individual to practice in the architectural profession. Thus, IDP is recognized by a majority of states' licensing authorities as a necessary element in the education of graduates of schools of architecture to be qualified to take the exam for licensure. The following represent two sample core competencies required by the IDP. (The IDP has a twenty-page booklet of core competencies you can download from www.e-architect.com/career/idp/corecomp.pdf.)

Building Cost Analysis   Building cost analysis involves the estimation of the project's probable construction cost. At the completion of your internship, you should be able to analyze and evaluate construction costs; prepare a building cost analysis that meets the program's requirements and provides alternatives for the owner or client; prepare preliminary cost analyses using unit cost/building type basis (cost per square foot); investigate and prepare quantity calculations for selected materials; research life-cycle cost information in relation to specifications; and factor the current inflation rate and other economic variables into the cost estimates.

Schematic Design   Schematic design involves the development of graphic alternative solutions to the program for the client's approval. At the completion of your internship, you should be able to develop alternative solutions to a specific program and document and present your solutions to a client for selection and approval.

In addition to these core competencies, you will have to know how to develop a project's program into alternative conceptual design proposals; evaluate engineering systems appropriate to the project; prepare volume and area calculations and evaluate the cost of alternative design proposals; prepare presentation drawings and models; review the schematic design with the client and revise the design based on the client's feedback; communicate the intent of the design orally, graphically, and in writing to facilitate the client's decision-making process; coordinate the consultants' activities relative to the schematic design; and incorporate relevant code requirements into the schematic design. If, upon graduation from your school of architecture, you are able to accomplish these and other core competencies required by the IDP, you will find yourself ready for licensure and practice of architecture.

RESIDENTIAL, COMMERCIAL, AND INSTITUTIONAL ARCHITECTURE

Architects hold about 99,000 jobs across North America. The majority of jobs are in architectural firms—most of which employ fewer than five workers. A few architects work for general building contractors or for government agencies responsible for housing, planning, or community development, such as the U.S. Departments of Defense and Interior, and the General Services Administration. About three in ten architects are self-employed.

Architects design a wide variety of buildings, including office and apartment buildings, schools, libraries, churches, factories, hospitals and health-care facilities, private residences, and airport terminals. They also design complexes such as urban centers, college campuses, industrial parks, and entire communities. They may also advise on the selection of building sites, prepare cost analysis and land-use studies, and do long-range planning for land development.

SPECIALIZING

Architects sometimes specialize in one phase of work. Some specialize in the design of one type of building—for example, hospitals and schools, or individual houses. Others focus on planning and predesign services or construction management and do little design work.

Architects often work with engineers, urban planners, interior designers, landscape architects, and others. (These related fields are discussed in later chapters.)

In this chapter we focus on firsthand accounts from architects doing residential, commercial, and institutional work. But first, here are a few sample job listings to give you an idea of what's out there. Because these are meant only as examples, hiring firms are not mentioned. You may find similar current listings by visiting the American Institute of Architects (AIA) website at www.aiaonline.com or conducting your own Internet search using keywords such as "architecture" and "jobs".

SAMPLE JOB LISTINGS

Architect/Designer, Wisconsin

A design firm is offering positions for passionate, ambitious graduates with two to three years minimum architectural experience, to work on all phases of single and multifamily residential, mixed-use commercial, institutional, and urban design projects.

Project Manager/Interiors, Colorado

An innovative and award-winning 160-person architecture and interiors firm is seeking talented individuals for exciting large-scale projects with hi-tech firms that are pushing the boundaries of traditional corporate architecture and redefining the work environment. An excellent opportunity to work in a collaborative atmosphere that advocates "whole building" thinking. Upcoming projects include corporate campuses that incorporate recreational facilities, restaurants, and shopping to create independent communities. Qualifications: five to seven years of experience; AutoCAD 13/14 2D proficiency preferred; excellent organizational skills; degree in interior design or architecture; interior design certification or architectural license preferred.

Architect, Missouri

Must be licensed and have three to five years' experience as architect. Position involves all aspects of health-care design and construction. Must have both verbal and writing skills and have working knowledge of AutoCAD 14 or 2000. Presentation skills preferred. Salary negotiable.

Forensic Architect, Oregon

National construction consulting firm seeking architect specializing in forensic investigation, construction defect litigation, and code interpretation. Comprehensive salary and benefits package offered.

Intermediate-Senior Level Architect, Texas

Architects with six to fifteen years' experience for quality community, recreation, library, and resort projects. Candidates must have general experience in architectural design, strong technical skills, and detailing expertise with Auto-CAD 14. Applicants must be responsive learners and strong team players. Intermediate technical staff is needed for preparation of design development and construction documents for Type-II and Type-V projects ranging from $3–50 million. Previous work in related project and building types and 3-D modeling a plus.

Library Architect, Washington

Library architect with five-plus years' experience in design, production, or project management of community or academic library projects to work in our expanding library practice. Candidate must have strong communication as well as graphic skills, experience leading design or production teams, and experience working with public and/or academic community user groups. Work experience must include strong technical, CAD, and teamwork skills. Previous work in related community or academic building types will be considered.

Staff Architect, Ohio

Immediate opportunity for a staff architect. Someone to help take a project from design development through construction. We specialize in designing and building prestigious senior retirement communities, therefore health-care experience would be appreciated! Proficiency in AutoCAD 14 is required, as is a professional degree with at least one year of experience. Registration is a plus, not a requirement.

FIRSTHAND ACCOUNTS

Joel André, Architect

Joel André is an architect and interior designer and owns his own firm called André Marquez Architects, located in Virginia Beach, Virginia. He has been practicing architecture since 1979, when he graduated from the School of Architecture at Pratt Institute in Brooklyn, New York. He has a Bachelor of Architecture degree.

In 1988 he passed the New York state licensing boards and became a licensed architect in the state of New York, and through reciprocity, acquired his Virginia license, allowing him to practice in Virginia.

Getting Started

"I became interested in this profession after being exposed to it by an uncle who was an architect. So, from a very young age, I can remember wanting to do what he did. As it turns out, between all the cousins and distant cousins, there are six other architects and a number of engineers in my family.

"I have always been fascinated with the ability to design a structure that will meet a specific human need. I have always enjoyed the problem-solving aspect of the profession.

"I got my first job in the profession when I came out of school, working for a local architect in New York who had also graduated from Pratt. It was a small firm specializing in renovation and use conversion in New York, but primarily in Park Slope, Brooklyn, which is a brownstone type of neighborhood that was in the process of becoming gentrified.

"The wonderful thing about working in this firm was that because it was so small, from the very beginning, I was able to get involved with the actual design of projects and be exposed to every facet of the profession.

"Some of the people I graduated with followed a different track. They went to large firms, where they were exposed to larger or more prominent projects, but did not get, in my opinion, the full exposure to the nuts and bolts of the business that I got, as fast as I got it. In the larger firms your growth is a bit slower, but the advantage is that you get to work on some major projects. There are pros and cons in either track.

"Four years ago I was in transition out of a position as a project architect in a firm in Virginia Beach, when I decided to take the plunge and start my own firm. Because of the relationships that I had in the profession and past clients I had remained in contact with, I was able to open my doors and hang my shingle without too much struggle. Because the firm I was working for closed its doors, there was no conflict in servicing some of their old clients. Like all new businesses, we go through some tight times, but on the average, we are doing better than would be expected."

What the Work Is Like

"Our clients include commercial, residential, churches, Department of Defense, as well as state and municipal organizations. Because of the diversity of our clients, the types of projects that we are involved with also tend to be varied. That makes the day-to-day aspect of the business very interesting. But the bottom line of this profession is that it is a service-oriented field. It requires a desire to serve people, because ultimately, most buildings that you will be involved in designing will be used by people to facilitate or meet a specific need."

A Typical Project

"To give you a broad-brush look at the practice of architecture, let me first run through the process for a typical project:

"One of the indispensable facets of the business of architecture is marketing. This involves following leads on who is planning to build or even earlier, who is thinking of building. If you do work for the state or federal government, this involves responding to Requests for Proposals (RFPs) that are published in special publications or advertised in the local papers.

"Once you respond to the advertisement requesting architectural services, there is a selection process that occurs, since there are generally several architectural firms pursuing these ads.

"Assuming you are selected, a contract is negotiated with the client, establishing the scope of the project and your fee for the services that you will provide. The contracts also establish the schedule in which the construction documents will be accomplished. These documents include the drawings, specifications, and the coordination of the other disciplines that are going to be involved in the project.

"Generally, these are other engineering fields, such as civil engineers for the site work, structural engineers for the foundations and structure framework of the building, the plumbing and mechanical—meaning heating and air-conditioning—and electrical engineers, and also the landscape architect, fire protection engineer for sprinkler systems, and any other special conditions that require input from a specialist, such as acoustical conditions or lighting conditions.

"The architect is responsible for the production of the documents that will be used by the builder or contractor to build the building. He is responsible for making sure that the program or the list of requirements and needs and functions that the building has to meet satisfies all the needs of the owner/user, from a functional point of view as well as for the safety and welfare of the occupants.

"He also must do all of this within budget—which often requires a reevaluation of the scope of the project to fit the budget or an adjustment of the budget to fit the scope. It is critical that this occur in the beginning stages of the project. You may design a great building, but if it can't be built because it exceeds the budget it is a bad experience for everyone. So a very important facet of this business is cost estimating.

"Once the scope of the project and the budget for the project have been reconciled and the architect has pulled together his team of consultants, we will launch into the concept design phase of the project. This is where the preliminary design work is done. We establish the general direction of the shape, volume, basic space layouts, and site layout, showing where on the site the building will sit. We take into consideration access, visibility, presentation to street, relationship to neighbors, solar orientation, drainage of site, utility connections, what the building will look like, with consideration for materials to be used, while complying with all the zoning and building codes applicable.

"During this phase and all the other phases of this process, we do a constant review of the cost and budget to make sure that the decisions being made in the design process are going to be buildable.

"Once the concept design has been reviewed and approved by the client, (this generally requires several presentations and revisions), then the project goes into the design development phase. This is where the design is refined, materials are selected, the engineer consultants are given directions to do their portion of the work, and the coordination of these various disciplines begins in earnest.

"At the end of this phase, the building design is finalized and as always the evaluation of the cost versus budget is done.

"From this phase, we proceed to the construction document production phase. This is where the construction drawings or blueprints are done, as well as the specifications that spell out in more detail the materials, the quality of the materials, the installation of these materials, and the maintenance of the materials, as well as the warranties for each material to be used in the building.

"The specifications complement the drawings in order to give the contractor all the information he will need to build the building as it is designed. This phase generally is the longest.

"While the architect is producing his drawings and specifications, his consultants are also producing their drawings and documents that will complement the architectural documents. These are added to the architectural drawing set, and their respective specification sections are added to the project specification book.

"Once the construction documents are completed, they are released so contractors interested in building the project can make their bids.

"Once a contractor has been selected, the responsibility of the architect is to make sure that the client is getting what he or she is paying for and that the contractor is using the materials and installing the equipment that were specified in the construction documents. At the same time, he has a responsibility to the contractor to make sure that he has all the information he needs to do his work.

"Once the building is completed and all systems are operational, the project is closed out, and the owner/user assumes occupancy of the building. Ideally, all parties are satisfied and we all part friends. This, I find, depends greatly on the individual players in this complex process. However, we do carry liability insurance.

"Generally, there are no typical days. Depending on which phase of a project you are in, you have specific goals you are working toward. And it gets even more interesting when you have several projects in various phases of development. This is where a good staff of designers, CAD operators, administrative staff, and project architects and project managers come into play.

"Also, depending on the types of projects you do, the approach to the work might vary. Some firms specialize in one building type, such as hospitals or hotels or residential.

"However, on the average, because of my position, I spend a lot of time coordinating the work that goes on in the office between the client, consultants, contractors, and all other interested parties. I also do the concept design for the projects. I want that initial input, establishing the direction of the design to the satisfaction of the client.

"This is a people profession. If my client isn't happy, I am not going to be happy since the client will find himself or herself another architect."

Upsides and Downsides "The upside of architecture is that it is a profession that will give you a view on your environment very different from most other professions. You will have an understanding of your environment that no other profession will give you.

"What I like most about practicing architecture is the creative aspect of the business. The design and problem-solving aspects are the things that I like to do. I love to design and conceptualize a client's vision into a product that fulfills that vision. I enjoy working out the details in the design development phase. Unfortunately, that is only about 10 to 15 percent of the whole process.

"I also enjoy the construction document phase of the work, the working drawings and the specifications, but not as much as the design.

"The part I enjoy the least is the administrative or business end of the profession. That was not why I became an architect, but it is an unavoidable part of the business. In fact, I would suggest that an M.B.A. would be an ideal post-graduate degree for architects. Either that or hire a good business manager. We have to wear so many hats as architects, trying to wing it as a businessperson can be deadly.

"I find that architecture affects every aspect of your life, because it does require a love for the profession to remain in it."

Salaries

"The financial rewards are not always there, especially when starting out. Most architects are not rich. I earn approximately $50,000 a year. My salary is based on the fees I negotiate with the client at the onset of the contract.

"An individual just out of school can expect to make anywhere from $22,000 to $28,000 per year. This varies depending on the geographic location and the state of the economy. Large cities tend to have higher salaries, but the cost of living is generally higher, so it is often a wash.

"A project manager, or project architect, who is licensed, can make approximately $32,000 to $50,000, again depending on the firm and the location. An established architect can earn anywhere from $50,000 to $150,000 a year and, in the larger firms with profit sharing and other benefit packages, the earnings can be even higher."

Advice from Joel André

"The primary requisites to be an architect are a good understanding of the profession and a love for the work. I say that because it does require a lot from you, often with small rewards, especially in the beginning.

"The qualities you'll need to be a good architect are good people skills, problem-solving skills, creativity, and an appreciation of the pure logic of engineering.

"For training, I would recommend a five-year school providing a professional degree, and practical office work during summer and winter breaks. Find an architect who will bring you in and maintain that relationship throughout your schooling. It's an incredible asset to have the right expectations of the profession when you come out of school, as opposed to stepping into the reality of everyday practice while your head is still in the clouds of academia.

"So to get started, I recommend you visit an architect's office or better yet, several offices, and if at all possible, spend a couple of weeks of a summer vacation while in your sophomore or junior year in an architect's office, even if you have to volunteer your time. Then, I would visit some architectural schools to get a good understanding of the profession.

"Ultimately, make sure it's something you really want to do, and understand the sacrifices it will require."

Judy Moore, Architect

Judy Moore is a self-employed architect (Judy Moore & Associates) in Albuquerque, New Mexico. She's involved in both residential and commercial projects and has been in the field since 1989. She earned her B.A. in architecture from the University of New Mexico.

Getting Started

"Originally, I was an art major (sculpture) but felt the competition too steep and the opportunities too few to actually make a go of it. I switched my major to architecture because it would be easier to support myself and I felt that there was a strong enough connection to sculpture to keep my creativity satisfied.

"I started doing residential remodel jobs when I was a sophomore in college to help pay for my education. The first few jobs were for relatives and friends of relatives. They did not pay very much, but the clients were patient with me and I really appreciated the opportunities to learn the things that would not be available to me through school.

"I started my own business in 1989 doing contract work for larger architectural firms and some residential projects for myself."

What the Work Is Like

"The residential work I do includes new construction (custom homes) and remodeling jobs, large and small. The commercial jobs include medical facilities, schools, and resorts/hotels.

"Currently, I am contracting work for a company that designs, builds, and remodels resort areas around the world. Each project has a five- or six-member team assigned to it. Each team travels to the particular job site to gather information for the preliminary design development phase (usually five to seven days, depending on the location).

"My duties vary from team to team and job to job. Most of the time I am the person responsible for preparing the construction documents for obtaining the building permits.

"During the project, I also participate in design development. I attend a weekly staff meeting during which each team provides an update for its particular project. Each week I also attend at least one team meeting for my project. During these meetings, we deal with unforeseen problems that have come up, and we review and sometimes revise our schedules to meet or change target dates for each phase of the project.

"Most of the time my work day is too short. I could use a couple more hours. The time passes quickly. I enjoy the work very much. Some weeks I work forty hours, some sixty hours, depending on deadlines."

Upsides and Downsides

"One of the things I've always liked about being an architect is learning about the specific uses and needs of each project, from playgrounds for handicapped children to hotels. Each project provides an opportunity to learn about the facilities and the people who work or live in them. Each comes with a set of design criteria that must be researched and developed.

"I enjoy the challenge of developing designs that meet the clients' goals and needs, while remaining within the constraints of a budget, the building codes, and the geographical site and its surroundings for the structure.

"Some of the things I like and dislike about my job are the same. On larger projects, I like it that someone else deals with the clients and manages the money. On smaller projects, I like dealing directly with the clients and managing the money myself.

"Small projects often involve working very closely with people wanting to build something they need (a spare room for an elderly parent needing home care, or a remodel of a very outdated kitchen). Their budgets are small and for that reason, I usually adjust my fee accordingly (to a point).

"Larger projects involve clients with larger budgets who are used to dealing with professionals and are willing to spend the money needed to get what they want.

"Each type of project, large and small, requires finding design solutions for specific problems, which is what I like to do. I like it because I'm good at it. It's easy to like something you're good at."

Salaries

"Currently, I earn around $90,000 annually. Of course, this amount varies as much as $10,000 depending on the number and kinds of contracts I get each year. And of course it took me ten years to build the client base for referrals and such. Right now I bill at an average rate of $40 per hour. That dollar amount varies according to the job."

Advice from Judy Moore

"If you are considering pursuing architecture as a career, you should enjoy the process of design and feel good about or proud of your solutions.

"There are no monetary guarantees. This profession, like many others, moves up and down with the economy. It is a tight community whose jobs are dependent on referrals and word of mouth and being in the right place at the right time."

Julie Haney, Architect

Julie Haney is a project architect with Ridge Builders Group, a design/build firm in Davis, California. She works with residential remodels and custom homes.

She earned her B.Arch. at Cal Poly, San Luis Obispo, California, and has been working in the field since 1990.

Getting Started

"I was really interested in art and math and wanted to combine the two; architecture was a perfect fit. I also felt that since I had to work for a living I wanted to do something that I enjoyed."

What the Work Is Like   "As a project architect in a design/build firm I experience every level of architecture, from the initial site visit/measurement meeting with the client, to the final walk-through at the end of the job.

"It is very rewarding to experience the sprouting of an idea all the way through to a physical, three-dimensional realization of that idea. Especially when the client is thrilled beyond his or her dreams!

"In order to achieve this, though, a lot must happen. There are two main phases: design and construction. Within the design phase there are three basic phases: programming and schematics, design development, and construction documentation.

"Phase one is where I meet with the client and review with him or her the estimate letter that outlines the project. (This was previously generated by one of our estimators.) Because I mostly work on remodels, I discuss the likes and dislikes of the existing situation or house with the client. The process evolves as I take the newly gathered information and turn it into a schematic design for the client to approve. This schematic design is also a springboard for generating ideas and eventually narrowing it into the final idea.

"Once the final schematic is approved, phase two starts—design development. During this phase the design is further developed, window and door sizes are established, as are the exterior elevations and general material selections. A mid-project estimate at this time is a good idea for a reality check on project costs. The end of phase two is marked by the design being developed to the point where the drawings and plans can go out to consultants for structural and Title 24 analysis (California energy code).

"During the time that the plans are at the consultants I usually continue meeting with the client to specify finish materials, plumbing and lighting fixtures, appliances, and so on.

"I begin to develop details, and once the drawings come back from the consultants, I incorporate all details and consultant work into the final set of drawings. This is reviewed by the client and then goes to the building department for plan check. The specifications are completed and given to the estimator along with a copy of the plans so that he or she can finalize the construction costs. This marks the end of phase three.

"After this I respond to plan check comments, attend a preconstruction meeting at the start of the remodel job, review shop drawings from the cabinetmaker, and make general site observations."

Upsides and Downsides   "I like the variety of job tasks that I do. I love specifying finish materials and coming up with designs. I love seeing the final project, as well as seeing the project grow.

"I love when my clients stand in awe and say 'this project is so wonderful that it has changed the quality my life.'

"But I hate indecisive clients who change their mind every day, or clients who get upset and don't know how to be civil when discussing their issues, or clients who expect me to read their mind and then get mad because I didn't foresee their inability to visualize after they claimed they completely understood their plans and specs."

Salaries

"I earn about $37,000 a year. Someone just starting out can expect to earn about $9 to $12 per hour, depending on location."

Advice from Julie Haney

"I think the main skills for an apprentice architect to develop are computer drafting, 3-D visualization, people and communication skills, the ability to sketch your ideas clearly and simply . . . and business sense.

"Obviously, education is the key here. Go to a reputable school that has a solid program or specializes in a field you are interested in. Especially look for a school that teaches commonsense thinking.

"I strongly recommend working in an architecture office during summer breaks or vacations. Most schools don't teach how to complete a full set of working drawings or other basics; they mostly concentrate on design and other useful things.

"There is a battery of tests you will have to take to become licensed after you graduate. There are local AIA chapters that can help guide you on this process.

"The job outlook depends on what field you are thinking about. If you are into designing elderly care facilities there will be lots of opportunities as the baby boomers age.

"Remodels have to continue to be plentiful as land becomes more precious. Community-oriented neighborhoods would be a great thing to see more of, especially if they are sustainable.

"Careers in solar and energy-efficient building design would have the greatest impact on the quality of the environment and future generations. But, as a professor or two told our classes, 'if you are in architecture for the money, get out of here and go to the business department!'

"As architects we are in part responsible for the built environment and how it impacts our natural resources as well as the human psyche. This is a big responsibility that should not be taken lightly. Through our creations we can make a difference."

HISTORIC PRESERVATION

A restoration architect—or an architect specializing in historic preservation—has much of a general architect's experience. He or she understands how to plan spaces, how to organize construction materials, and how to put together construction documents.

The difference between a general architect and a restoration architect is that the latter's work experience has primarily been focused on historic buildings. In addition, the restoration architect will have a specialized knowledge and understanding of federal, state, and local regulations with regard to historic preservation. He or she will also be aware of the standards set by the particular style of architecture.

PRESERVATION CATEGORIES

The activity of preservation includes several different categories. Adaptive reuse is when architects provide a new function for older structures that would otherwise be demolished. For example, a defunct mill is converted into an office building or a college. Architectural conservation involves using special techniques to halt further deterioration of building materials. Restoration, which may be called "historical restoration," involves the meticulous return of a building to its former appearance at a particular period in history. Rehabilitation or renovation involves altering or upgrading existing buildings and structures.

RELATED FIELDS

There are several related fields: architectural historians, architectural conservators, curators of structures, and other preservationists, who all share a love of historic buildings and architecture. They might specialize in a particular period or style, fascinated by Victorian gingerbread, strong red brick or federal woodwork, and old frame farmhouses and barns. Most, however, are generalists, possessing knowledge that crosses the centuries. These professionals are good researchers or artists and have strong organizational skills and an interest in the environment as well as history.

ARCHITECTURAL CONSERVATORS

Architectural conservators are not necessarily registered architects. They might have started out in the construction and contracting field, gaining along the way specialized technical experience in problems that occur with historic buildings. Some of these problems involve the historic building fabric such as cracks in foundations and walls, water seepage, and how to clean the building. They understand how buildings were constructed during earlier periods, and know what kinds of complications result from the natural course of time and different climatic and environmental conditions. They are familiar with building materials, roofs, windows, exterior cladding, and various construction types, such as wood frame or masonry-clad structures.

Architectural conservators are also sometimes known as curators of structures.

ARCHITECTURAL HISTORIANS

Architectural historians are historians with an interest in architecture. They are generally not registered architects. They often work with restoration architects, however, conducting specialized investigations and performing all the research necessary to get a restoration project underway. They dig up a building's history—when it was constructed, what its original purpose was, how long it was vacant, whether any changes had been made. They then put together a historic structures report for the architect who wants to make his or her restoration work as accurate as possible.

Architectural historians can work in academic settings, for private architectural firms, and for government agencies concerned with historic preservation. The minimum educational requirement for an architectural historian is an undergraduate degree in history or architectural history, although most positions require a graduate degree.

HISTORIC INTERIOR DESIGNERS

To achieve complete authenticity, the interior of a historic building must be given as much attention as the exterior, especially if the building will be used as a museum open to the public. Historic interior designers can be architects or specially trained professionals. They must be experienced in the investigation, documentation, research, and analysis of the lighting, furnishings, finishes, and decorative arts of building interiors. Historic interior specialists generally work as part of a team with the restoration architect and conservator.

ASSOCIATIONS INVOLVED WITH HISTORIC PRESERVATION

These organizations are listed here because their work involves historic preservation. They depend on membership to stay alive, and would encourage anyone with an interest in this area to join. They also provide jobs to restoration architects.

National Trust for Historic Preservation

The National Trust for Historic Preservation is a nonprofit organization, chartered by Congress in 1949, now with more than 250,000 individual members. It is dedicated to protecting the irreplaceable. It fights to save historic buildings and the neighborhoods and landscapes they anchor. The National Trust's mission is, indeed, to preserve and revitalize the livability of our communities by leading the nation in saving America's historic environments. It provides technical advice and financial assistance to nonprofit organizations and public agencies engaged in preservation, as well as to the general public. The National Trust also acts as an advocate for protection of the country's heritage in the courts and with legislative and regulatory agencies.

Through education and advocacy, the National Trust is revitalizing communities across the country and challenges citizens to create sensible plans for the future. It has six regional offices, twenty historic sites, and works with thousands of local community groups nationwide. Most of the National Trust's funding comes from membership dues, corporation and foundation grants, endowment income, and merchandise sales. About 22 percent comes from a matching grant awarded by the U.S. Congress through the U.S. Department of the Interior. The National Trust believes that the employment outlook in the historic preservation field has grown dramatically over the past decade. Its concerns have enlarged from a relatively small number of historic sites, museums, and buildings to historic neighborhoods, commercial districts, and rural landscapes.

The growing sophistication of the field is reflected in the greater diversity of professionals who contribute to preservation work. Historians, curators, and other museum professionals are now joined by architects, lawyers, designers, realtors, planners, developers, mortgage lenders, and others. Once found working only in museums, libraries, and historical societies, preservationists now are also employed in real estate firms that specialize in historical properties, and in financial institutions that invest in older neighborhoods.

The National Trust employs many specialists in its national office in Washington and in its seven regional offices. In addition, the National Trust owns and operates eighteen historic house museums. It also publishes *Historic Preserva-*

tion magazine and *Historic Preservation News*, which are distributed to members. The latter lists job opportunities and internships within both the National Trust and outside organizations.

For more information, write to:

National Trust for Historic Preservation
1785 Massachusetts Avenue NW
Washington, DC 20036
www.htnp.org

U.S. Artifacts Recovery Association—National Association for the Preservation of Historical Artifacts

By connecting with other associations, individuals, government agencies, and others, the U.S. Artifacts Recovery Association feels it can save more history than by doing it separately.

Their mission statement is "With ever advancing construction, many historical artifacts are lost forever, to us all. We are committed to the preservation of these historical artifacts, and believe that the vast majority of Americans share our thoughts."

The Association for Preservation Technology International (APT)

The Association for Preservation Technology International (APT) is a multidisciplinary organization dedicated to "advancing the application of technology to the conservation of the built environment." Members of APT include architects, conservators, consultants, contractors, craftspersons, curators, developers, educators, engineers, historians, landscape architects, managers, planners, preservationists, technicians, tradespeople, and others involved in the systematic application of the knowledge of methods and materials to the conservation of buildings, districts, and artifacts.

ICOMOS

ICOMOS is an international nongovernmental organization of professionals, dedicated to the conservation of the world's historic monuments and sites. The U.S. National Committee of the International Council on Monuments and Sites (US/ICOMOS) fosters heritage conservation and historic preservation at the national and international levels through education and training, international exchange of people and information, technical assistance, documentation, advocacy, and other activities consistent with the goals of ICOMOS and through collaboration with other organizations.

US/ICOMOS membership includes professionals, practitioners, supporters, and organizations committed to the protection, preservation, and conservation of the world's cultural heritage. ICOMOS is UNESCO's principal advisor in matters concerning the conservation and protection of monuments and sites.

With IUCN–The World Conservation Union, ICOMOS has an international role under the World Heritage Convention to advise the World Heritage Committee and UNESCO on the nomination of new sites to the World Heritage List.

Through its sixteen International Scientific Committees of experts from around the world, and through its triennial General Assembly, ICOMOS seeks to establish international standards for the preservation, restoration, and management of the cultural environment. Many of these standards have been promulgated as Charters by the organization as a result of adoption by the ICOMOS General Assembly. ICOMOS activities are governed by a set of statutes that were adopted by the Fifth General Assembly in Moscow on May 22, 1978. For more information, contact www.icomos.org/usicomos.

Federal Highway Administration

The Federal Highway Administration has an awards program for preservation projects, particularly for historic bridges. The National Historic Covered Bridge Preservation (NHCBP) program was established by Section 1224 of the Transportation Equity Act for the 21st Century (TEA21). The program provides funding to assist the states in their efforts to preserve, rehabilitate, or restore the nation's historic covered bridges. For the purposes of this program, the term "historic covered bridge" means a covered bridge that is listed or eligible for listing on the National Register for Historic Places. Contact: www.fhwa.dot.gov/bridge/covered.htm.

National Register of Historic Places

The National Register of Historic Places is the nation's official list of cultural resources worthy of preservation. Authorized under the National Historic Preservation Act of 1966, the National Register is part of a national program to coordinate and support public and private efforts to identify, evaluate, and protect our historic and archaeological resources.

Properties listed in the Register include districts, sites, buildings, structures, and objects that are significant in American history, architecture, archaeology, engineering, and culture. The National Register is administered by the National Park Service, which is part of the U.S. Department of the Interior.

The official website of the National Register of Historic Places provides a searchable database of properties on the U.S. National Register, educational resources, National Historic Preservation Act requirements, preservation information resources, and virtual tours of historic sites. Contact: www.cr.nps.gov/nr.

FIRSTHAND ACCOUNTS

Gary Fischer, Architect

Gary Fischer is the principal with Arkinetics Inc., an architectural firm in Lorain and Cleveland, Ohio. Arkinetics is a general practice firm, handling historic preservation and adaptive reuse as well as some limited custom residential, commercial, and industrial work.

He received a B.S. and a B.Arch. from Kent State University, with an emphasis on historic preservation, renovation, and adaptive reuse. He has been working in the field since 1984 and received NCARB certification in the early 1990s.

Getting Started

"I first became interested in the field of architecture during a sixth-grade career day program. I thought it would be fun to draw buildings and to see them constructed. After graduation from college I interviewed with several large firms (one-hundred-plus people) and several smaller ones (one or two people). I was offered a job with a very large firm that designed mostly malls and retail stores. I knew that the pay would be more than adequate, but I thought that the work would be boring, so I decided against taking the job. I then went back to a small, one-man firm that did more creative work and convinced them to hire me.

"I served my three-year apprenticeship working there and helped the owner increase the size of the firm to seven people. During that time I was studying for my five-day licensing test so I would actually become a Registered Architect. One afternoon, the owner announced that he would never make another architect a partner. Since there was a limited future at that company, I began to plan starting up my own firm with two other employees who felt the same way I did. We discussed leaving with our boss and assured him that we would not steal his clients and would be willing to assist him in easing the transition caused by our departure. We staggered our departure dates so that he could bring in new employees.

"After almost a year of planning our company, Arkinetics, was born. Our first project was a building renovation."

What the Work Is Like

"Today, my job is to act as a principal of Arkinetics. It is not the least bit boring. I start a typical week by making out the work assignment schedule for the draftspeople. In this meeting we discuss the status of each project and its expected completion date. After that I might leave the office to meet with the contractor(s) on a construction site and observe their work. Later I might tour an existing office, store, or factory to prepare a proposal for a client in need of more space or a renovation. I frequently interview people to discuss their needs for a project. I prepare design sketches and color drawings for clients to review and make presentations to clients, city government, planning boards, and civic groups.

"In general, architects work between forty and sixty hours per week. The job can be highly stressful at times because of tight project schedules or difficulties during the construction process.

"Our projects range from recreating an authentic barn with modern conveniences (hidden of course) to be used as a park visitor center in a historic park, to high-tech corporate offices and industrial buildings for a variety of companies. Visiting the facilities is one of the most interesting parts of my job. I have watched automotive parts being assembled and seen injection molders creating parts for a costume in a Disney movie. We have designed parks along the shores of Lake Erie, renovated two historic buildings to be used as home recording studios, designed loft-style apartments in old commercial buildings, and helped to create an entirely new community for 450 new homes and shops in the heart of a depressed community. On one occasion I was interviewed for a PBS video about the construction of a local historic monument.

"Because we are under such pressure to meet deadlines I like to keep the office atmosphere friendly and light. We all pitch in like a team to accomplish our work. It's stressful, but fun. The least enjoyable parts of my job are the evening board meetings and the tight time schedules."

Salaries

"A principal in a large firm could earn upwards of $100,000 a year. Most architects earn on average $30,000 to $70,000 a year, but the starting salary could be as low as $25,000. Salaries are based on skills—better skills, better pay."

Advice from Gary Fischer

"To be a successful architect, you should possess dedication, good verbal and written communication skills, imagination, and a love of creativity. Be prepared for five grueling years of college. While you watch your friends go home for the weekend or out with friends, you will be completing a project for a class deadline. At those times the decision you make will determine whether you really have the dedication to become an architect.

"Math, physics, and art courses in high school will help in the college years. And remember to draw and sketch as much as possible. I started with a class of about 190 students in my freshman year at Kent. Forty students graduated after five years. Several went on to easier fields at the urging of the professors . . . they became doctors!"

Peter Benton, Architect

Pete Benton is a restoration architect, specializing in historic preservation. He earned a B.S. in architecture in 1972 from the University of Virginia in Charlottesville. He worked for several years for various firms in Philadelphia and Washington, D.C., then went on to complete his M.Arch. from the University of Pennsylvania in 1979.

Getting Started

"Initially, I had relatively little training in preservation, but I was exposed to the idea of ecological planning at UPenn. I saw the philosophical connection between an ecological approach to the landscape and to the buildings, and that led me to historic preservation. I went to work for four or five years for an ecological planning firm, and it was there my interest developed further.

"I am now a senior associate with John Milner and Associates, Inc., a midsize architectural firm in West Chester, Pennsylvania, specializing in historic preservation. I joined the staff in 1984 and have worked on a variety of projects."

What the Work Is Like

"I've been responsible for all sorts of properties—anything from small, privately owned residential-scale houses from the eighteenth century to high-style nineteenth-century mansions. In addition, I've worked with historic commercial and industrial buildings from the nineteenth century, restoring them or practicing what we call adaptive reuse. For example, we recently converted an old mill into an office building and a farmhouse into a meeting facility.

"Another category I've worked with includes monumental buildings, such as a city hall, or large federal buildings.

"First I meet with the client and determine what his or her goals for the property are. Then I do an existing conditions analysis of the site, look at the historical development of the building over time, take photographs, field measurements, and written notes.

"Next I do a schematic plan, making preliminary drawings and sketches, describing a design to the client for the client's approval. This stage could take four weeks or so. Once the client approves the project, I produce an outline of the scope of work and figure an order-of-magnitude cost estimate.

"After that stage is approved, the next phase is to work on design development documents. This involves the use of more detailed drawings and can take from six to eight weeks. Over the next eight to twelve weeks construction documents including drawings and specifications are produced. During the bidding phase, the contractor is selected. Then if necessary, we review and revise the construction plans before actually beginning work. I make frequent visits to the site while the project is in progress.

"Construction time varies but could take eight months or a year and a half depending upon the scope of the project."

Salaries

"Someone fresh from graduate school can expect to earn from $25,000 to $27,000 per year, depending of course upon the size of the firm, the importance of the project, and the region of the country. Advancement would depend upon your ability and accomplishments.

"An experienced architect with five years or more at the project manager level could expect to earn about $40,000 a year in a mid-size firm. Those with specializations in demand can earn more."

**Advice from
Peter Benton**

"Most firms offer paid internships for graduate students, and it is a good idea to set one up for yourself. It gives you a foot in the door when it comes time to make arrangements for a full-time job when you graduate."

TEACHING ARCHITECTURE

The discipline of architecture is rooted in an understanding of the history of the field, its role in cultural development, and the ideas that shape architects and architecture. Some architects choose the pursuit of these roots as their life's work. This decision almost always requires advanced education, increasingly at the doctoral level, and leads to teaching and research appointments in architecture schools, art and cultural history departments, or museums and academies dedicated to the development of the field.

As we learned in Chapter 2, there are currently 123 schools in the United States and ten in Canada offering professional programs in architecture leading to the Bachelor of Architecture or Master of Architecture degree. (For a full list, see Appendix C.) In those 133 schools, 15,312 students are enrolled in full-time B.Arch. accredited programs and 1,606 are enrolled as part-time students. There are also 5,769 full-time M.Arch. candidates and 689 part-time master's-level students. There are also approximately 100 schools offering nonprofessional one- or two-year programs in architectural studies or technology.

All those students need teachers. According to the National Architectural Accrediting Board, currently there are 1,869 full-time faculty and 2,302 part-time. To give you an idea of the scope of teaching architecture, here is a breakdown of those numbers, prepared by the National Architectural Accrediting Board.

Full-Time Faculty Totals	1,869
Women	388
African-American	82
Native American	3
Asian/Pacific Isle	77
Hispanic	94

Part-Time Faculty Totals	**2,302**
Women	536
African-American	42
Native American	2
Asian/Pacific Isle	71
Hispanic	92
Total Tenured Faculty	**1,256**
Women	175
African-American	36
Native American	1
Asian/Pacific Isle	35

JOB OUTLOOK FOR ARCHITECTURE FACULTY

Between 1998 and 2008, the traditional college-age population (eighteen to twenty-four years of age) will grow again after several years of decline. This population increase, along with a higher proportion of eighteen- to twenty-four-year-olds attending college and a growing number of part-time, female, minority, and older students, will spur college enrollments. Enrollment is projected to rise from 14.6 million in 1998 to 16.1 million in 2008, an increase of about 10 percent.

Growing numbers of students will necessitate hiring more faculty members to teach them. At the same time, many faculty members will be retiring, opening up even more positions. Also, the number of doctoral degrees is expected to grow more slowly than in the past, somewhat easing the competition for some faculty positions.

Despite expected job growth and the need to replace retiring faculty, many in the academic community are concerned that institutions will increasingly favor the hiring of adjunct faculty over full-time, tenure-track faculty. For many years, keen competition for faculty jobs forced some applicants to accept part-time academic appointments that offered little hope of tenure, and others to seek nonacademic positions.

Many colleges, faced with reduced state funding for higher education and growing numbers of part-time and older students, increased the hiring of part-time faculty to save money on pay and benefits and to accommodate the needs of nontraditional-age students. If funding remains tight over the projection period, this trend of hiring adjunct or part-time faculty is likely to continue. Because of uncertainty about future funding sources, some colleges and universities are also controlling costs by changing the mix of academic programs offered, eliminating some programs altogether, and increasing class size. Even if the proportion of full-time positions does not shrink, job competition will remain keen for coveted tenure-track jobs. Some institutions are expected to increasingly hire full-time faculty on limited-term contracts, reducing the number of tenure-track positions available.

Overall, job prospects will continue to be better in certain fields—business, architecture, engineering, health science, and computer science, for example— that offer attractive nonacademic job opportunities and attract fewer applicants for academic positions. Also, excellent job prospects in a field—for example, engineering—result in higher student enrollments, increasing faculty needs in that field. In addition, nonresidential construction is expected to grow more quickly through 2008 than during the previous decade, driving demand for more architects. And when there is a need for more architects, there is a need for more architectural instructors.

WHO TEACHES ARCHITECTURE

That old saying, "those who can, do; those who can't, teach," couldn't be further from the truth when it comes to architecture. Many faculty members start out as practicing architects, then either leave the field full-time to teach, or supplement their work with part-time teaching. (Conversely, some part-time faculty members who have not yet landed full-time, tenure-track positions do design or other related work to supplement their income.) Still others have retired from full-time architecture work and act as consultants or become faculty members. For the most part, all university faculty members in architecture must have had real-time field experience before they can find employment teaching students.

FACULTY RESPONSIBILITIES

According to a study conducted by the NAAB, full-time faculty average 15.98 student contact hours per week, and those working part-time average 8.74 contact hours. In addition to class time and student consultation, faculty members may serve on academic or administrative committees that deal with the policies of their institution, departmental matters, academic issues, curricula, budgets, equipment purchases, and hiring. Some also work with student and community organizations outside the classroom.

Every college and university faculty must have a head of each concentration offered at the school. These important people oversee the curriculum and courses offered in their area—this includes the faculty members—and report to the dean of the college or university. These people are called department chairpersons, and they are faculty members who may teach some courses but usually have heavier administrative and managerial responsibilities.

The proportion of time spent on research, teaching, administrative, and other duties varies by individual circumstance and type of institution. Faculty members at universities normally spend a significant part of their time doing research; those in four-year colleges, somewhat less; and those in two-year colleges, relatively little. The teaching load, however, often is heavier in two-year colleges and somewhat lower at four-year institutions. Full professors at all types of institutions usually spend a larger portion of their time conducting research than do assistant professors, instructors, and lecturers.

Faculty members may instruct undergraduate or graduate students, or both. They may give lectures to several hundred students in large halls, lead small seminars, or supervise students in design studios. They prepare lectures, exercises, and assignments; grade exams and papers; and advise and work with students individually. In universities, they also supervise graduate students' teaching and research. College faculty members work with an increasingly varied student population made up of growing shares of part-time, older, and culturally and racially diverse students.

Faculty keep abreast of developments in their field by reading current literature, talking with colleagues, and participating in professional conferences. They may also conduct their own research to expand knowledge in their field.

SALARIES FOR ARCHITECTURE FACULTY

Most college and university faculty members can be categorized into four - academic ranks: professor, associate professor, assistant professor, and instructor. These positions are usually considered to be tenure-track positions. A small number of faculty members, called lecturers, are not usually on the tenure track.

According to an NAAB study, architecture faculty members have average annual earnings as listed below:

PROFESSORS

National Average	$67,239
Public Institution	66,992
Private Institution	67,704

ASSOCIATE PROFESSORS

National Average	$52,271
Public Institution	52,118
Private Institution	52,570

ASSISTANT PROFESSORS

National Average	$42,725
Public Institution	43,065
Private Institution	42,023

Earnings vary according to faculty rank and type of institution, geographic area, and field. According to a 1998–99 survey by the American Association of University Professors, salaries for full-time faculty across all fields averaged $56,300. By rank, the average for professors was $72,700; associate professors, $53,200; assistant professors, $43,800; instructors, $33,400; and lecturers, $37,200. Faculty in four-year institutions earn higher salaries, on the average, than those in two-year schools. Average salaries for faculty in public institutions—$55,900—were lower in 1998–99 than those for private independent institutions—$63,500—but higher than those for religiously affiliated private colleges and universities—$49,400. In fields with high-paying nonacademic alternatives—notably medicine and law but also engineering and business, among others—earnings exceed these averages. In others—such as the humanities and education—they are lower.

Most faculty members have significant earnings in addition to their base salary, from consulting, teaching additional courses, researching, writing for publication, or other employment. In addition, most enjoy some unique benefits, including access to campus facilities, tuition waivers for dependents, housing and travel allowances, and paid sabbatical leaves. Conversely, part-time faculty usually have fewer benefits, including health insurance, retirement benefits, and sabbatical leave, than full-time faculty. Because of this, some colleges and universities may attempt to cut costs by employing more part-time faculty members than full-time.

TRAINING FOR UNIVERSITY FACULTY

Four-year colleges and universities generally hire doctoral degree holders for full-time, tenure-track positions, but may hire master's degree holders or doctoral candidates for certain disciplines or for part-time and temporary jobs.

Doctoral programs usually take four to seven years of full-time study beyond the bachelor's degree. Programs include increasingly specialized courses and seminars plus comprehensive examinations on all major areas of the field. They also include a dissertation, a report on original research to answer some significant question in the field.

FINDING THAT JOB

Special publications on higher education, available in libraries and on-line, such as *The Chronicle of Higher Education*, list specific employment opportunities for faculty. Also, contact the specific institution in which you are interested to learn about openings, but be prepared to relocate. With only 133 accredited institutions in North America, chances are you'll have to move to find work.

SAMPLE JOB LISTINGS

These listings are provided as a sample only and as such, the hiring firms are not mentioned. You may find similar job listings by visiting websites for *The Chronicle of Higher Education* (www.chronicle.com) and related professional associations, or by performing an Internet search using keywords such as "university," "teaching," "jobs," and "architecture."

Assistant Professor—School of Landscape Architecture Education

Requirements: Applicants must hold an advanced degree; at least one degree must be from an accredited program in landscape architecture. The Ph.D. degree, or an interdisciplinary degree, is highly desirable. Fluency in a foreign language is beneficial. Professional registration, though not required, is advantageous.

The School of Landscape Architecture invites applications for a tenure-track, academic-year appointment at the Assistant Professor level. The successful applicant will teach courses in Landscape Planning and Geographic Information Systems, as well as other areas within the professional curriculum. The School of Landscape Architecture is one of three units in the College of Architecture, Planning, and Landscape Architecture (CAPLA). The graduate professional program offers the Master of Landscape Architecture degree as an accredited, three-year curriculum. Current enrollment is approximately fifty graduate students.

Assistant Professor—Department of Architecture

Minimum qualification: Master of Architecture degree, or master's degree in a related field with curriculum equivalency. Preferred qualifications: registration (license to practice architecture), quality of design work and/or evidence of contributions to the profession through practice and service; record of previous teaching experience and commitment to work in a collaborative environment; publications and/or appropriate research work as evidence of scholarly contributions.

Responsibilities: teaching design studios and courses in computer design; providing leadership in developing the curriculum in the area of computational tools for designing.

Architecture/Urban Planning

Requirements: Applicants must have a professional degree and a master's degree in an appropriate specialty with a minimum of three years' experience in professional practice and/or teaching experience at the undergraduate level. Preferences will be given to applicants with a Ph.D. degree or equivalent. Applicants in Urban Planning must have a Ph.D. Applicants must be able to show evidence of quality design production and an active and ongoing research agenda.

The Department of Architecture and Design has openings in Architecture and Urban Planning for the upcoming academic year, including continuing appointments and visiting positions for two semesters' duration. Salary and rank are commensurate with qualifications.

FIRSTHAND ACCOUNT

John Downs, Professor

John Downs is a full professor at a prestigious architecture institution in New York City. The courses he has taught over the years include basic and advanced design courses, architectural materials, structure, architectural history, cultural history, planning, construction documentation, and a range of electives.

He earned his B.Arch. in 1967 and his Ph.D. in 1977.

Getting Started

"A bachelor's in architecture is not necessary to go on for further study at the doctorate level. I was interested in doing research that was more humanistic than applied.

"A fellow student who had a job told me of their search for a new faculty member. I was not satisfied with the working conditions where I was. I was still writing my Ph.D. dissertation and felt that this new university would be a hospitable place to finish it. I was supporting a wife and child at the time and needed a job that would provide income as well as a relaxed atmosphere in which I could finish writing up my field research. The university where I was working before had no interest in advancing the instructors and put a heavy teaching load on them."

What the Work Is Like

"A university job in architecture is very much like a job with a professional program in any other field. The nature of the job depends much more on the institution for which you work than on the discipline in which you teach.

"The most coveted jobs at universities are the ones that lead to tenure. Tenure guarantees that the person will not be fired for teaching what he or she feels is right; however the person has to prove the quality of his or her teaching and scholarship before being granted tenure. This usually takes five or more years.

"Before getting tenure, a faculty member usually has to work very hard proving that he or she can produce scholarship of a quality that gets his or her work published in good journals. Very innovative and creative ideas are often appreciated by one's peers, but they may not be recognized in the tenure-granting process. Quality teaching is important.

"Before and after tenure university faculty people work very hard. They are usually very dedicated to their job. They may concentrate on doing new research, setting up academic programs, supervising student research, or teaching. There is a great opportunity to know students and help them mature personally and professionally. Many faculty members find great rewards in this.

"I usually spend ten or twelve hours a day doing something related to my job. I work as much as I can without jeopardizing my family life or friendships. This means that I usually work at something in the evening or on the weekends. It is often hard to define the boundary between work and leisure.

"The least pleasant part of my work is the bureaucratic requirements of my job. These do not bother everyone, and many faculty members enjoy participating in the bureaucratic structure of the university. The pleasantness of the bureaucracy can vary from university to university. Fortunately, I do not work for a university in which strong management has got the upper hand and treats the faculty like stupid employees. It may sound ridiculous, but there is a tendency in American universities for 'professional,' rather academically untrained administrations to develop. They pay less and less attention to the academic values of the university, and life can be made miserable for everyone. It is important to work for a university in which academic values, which include positive experiences for students, are put first.

"I don't like to give exams and hand out grades. I would like all my students to be fascinated by the subject matter and do the best they can, but, alas, they have varied goals and interests. Human nature places limits on the freedom that one can give to students and therefore the structure of teaching can be a burden at times."

Salaries

"One starting out can expect to earn around $30,000 per year. Salaries can go up to $70,000 and into six figures at the most wealthy and prestigious universities. The skills held by most faculty can bring in twice as much in the professional world if used competitively."

Advice from John Downs

"Check to see what the unemployment level is for the degree you are pursuing. Architecture could have a rather high level of Ph.D. unemployment. Be honest in examining your motives. Ask yourself if you are willing to put up with long years of graduate education, long years of field work, and then long years of job hunting—and you may have to move in order to secure a desirable position."

Part Two
Related Fields

LANDSCAPE ARCHITECTURE

Everyone enjoys attractively designed residential areas, public parks, college campuses, shopping centers, golf courses, parkways, and industrial parks. Landscape architects design these areas so that they are not only functional but beautiful and compatible with the natural environment as well. They may plan the location of buildings, roads, and walkways and the arrangement of flowers, shrubs, and trees. Historic preservation and natural resource conservation and reclamation are other important objectives to which landscape architects may apply their knowledge of the environment as well as their design and artistic talents.

Landscape architects are hired by many types of organizations—from real estate development firms starting new projects to municipalities constructing airports or parks. They are often involved with the development of a site from its conception. Working with architects, engineers, scientists, and other professionals, they help determine the best arrangement of roads and buildings, and the best way to conserve or restore natural resources. Once these decisions are made, landscape architects create detailed plans indicating new topography, vegetation, walkways, and landscape amenities.

In planning a site, landscape architects first consider the nature and purpose of the project and the funds available. They analyze the natural elements of the site, such as the climate, soil, slope of the land, drainage, and vegetation. They observe where sunlight falls on the site at different times of the day and examine the site from various angles. They assess the effect of existing buildings, roads, walkways, and utilities on the project.

After studying and analyzing the site, they prepare a preliminary design. To account for the needs of the client as well as the conditions at the site, they may have to make many changes before a final design is approved. They must also take into account any local, state, or federal regulations, such as those protecting wetlands or historic resources.

An increasing number of landscape architects are using computer-aided design (CAD) systems to assist them in preparing their designs. Many landscape architects also use video simulation as a tool to help clients envision the proposed ideas and plans. For larger-scale site planning, landscape architects also use geographic information systems technology, a computer mapping system.

Throughout all phases of the planning and design, landscape architects consult with other professionals involved in the project. Once the design is complete, they prepare a proposal for the client. They produce detailed plans of the site, including written reports, sketches, models, photographs, land-use studies, and cost estimates, and submit them for approval by the client and by regulatory agencies. If the plans are approved, landscape architects prepare working drawings showing all existing and proposed features. They also outline in detail the methods of construction and draw up a list of necessary materials. Although many landscape architects supervise the installation of their design, some are involved in the construction of the site. In general, however, this work is done by the developer or landscape contractor.

Some landscape architects work on a wide variety of projects. Others specialize in a particular area, such as residential development, historic landscape restoration, waterfront improvement projects, parks and playgrounds, or shopping centers. Still others work in regional planning and resource management; feasibility, environmental impact, and cost studies; or site construction. Some landscape architects teach in colleges or universities.

Although most landscape architects do at least some residential work, relatively few limit their practice to landscape design for individual homeowners. The reason for this is because most residential landscape design projects are too small to provide suitable income compared with larger commercial or multi-unit residential projects. For these kinds of smaller projects, some nurseries offer residential landscape design services. However, these services often are performed by less qualified landscape designers or others with training and experience in related areas.

Landscape architects who work for government agencies do similar work at national parks, government buildings, and other government-owned facilities. In addition, they may prepare environmental impact statements and studies on environmental issues such as public land-use planning. All landscape architects combine their knowledge of design, construction, plants, soils, and ecology to create their final designs.

WORKING CONDITIONS

Landscape architects spend most of their time in offices creating plans and designs, preparing models and cost estimates, doing research, or attending meetings. The remainder of their time is spent at the site. During the design and planning stage, landscape architects visit and analyze the site to verify that the design can be incorporated into the landscape. After the plans and specifications are completed, they may spend additional time at the site observing or supervising the construction. Those who work in large firms may spend considerably more time out of the office because of travel to sites outside the local area. Salaried employees in both government and landscape architectural firms usually work regular hours, although they may work overtime to meet a project deadline, whereas hours of self-employed landscape architects may vary from project to project.

EMPLOYMENT FIGURES

Landscape architects hold more than 22,000 jobs nationwide. About one out of two salaried workers are employed in firms that provide landscape architecture services, with architectural and engineering firms employing most of the rest. The federal government also employs these workers, primarily in the U.S. Departments of Agriculture, Defense, and Interior. About two of every five landscape architects are self-employed. Most landscape architects find work in urban and suburban areas throughout the country, although some landscape architects work in rural areas, particularly those in the federal government who plan and design parks and recreation areas.

JOB OUTLOOK

According to the U.S. Bureau of Labor Statistics, employment of landscape architects is expected to increase as fast as the average for all occupations through the year 2008. The level of new construction plays an important role in determining demand for landscape architects. Increased development of open space into recreation areas, wildlife refuges, and parks will also require the skills of landscape architects. Overall, anticipated growth in construction is expected to increase demand for landscape architectural services over the long run.

The recent passage of the Transportation Equity Act for the Twenty-First Century is expected to spur employment for landscape architects, particularly in state and local governments. This act, known as TEA21, provides funds for surface transportation and transit programs, such as interstate highway maintenance and environment-friendly pedestrian and bicycle trails. However, opportunities will vary from year to year and by geographic region, depending on local economic conditions. During a recession, when real estate sales and construction slow down, landscape architects may face layoffs and greater competition for jobs. The need to replace landscape architects who retire or leave the labor force for other reasons is expected to produce nearly as many job openings as employment growth.

An increasing proportion of office and other commercial and industrial development will occur outside cities. These projects are typically located on larger sites with more surrounding land that needs to be designed by a landscape architect, in contrast to urban development, which often includes little or no surrounding land.

Also, as the cost of land rises, the importance of good site planning and landscape design grows. Increasingly, new development is contingent upon compliance with environmental regulations and land use zoning, spurring demand for landscape architects to help plan sites and integrate man-made structures with the natural environment in the least disruptive way.

Budget tightening in the federal government might restrict hiring in the Forest Service and the National Park Service, agencies that traditionally employ the most landscape architects in the federal government. Instead, such agencies may increasingly contract out for landscape architecture services, providing additional employment opportunities in private landscape architecture firms.

In addition to the work related to new development and construction, landscape architects are expected to be involved in historic preservation, land reclamation, and refurbishment of existing sites. Because landscape architects can work on many different types of projects, they may have an easier time than other design professionals finding employment when traditional construction slows down.

New graduates can expect to face competition for jobs in the largest and most prestigious landscape architecture firms. The number of professional degrees awarded in landscape architecture has remained steady over the years, even during times of fluctuating demand due to economic conditions. Opportunities will be best for landscape architects who develop strong technical and communication skills and a knowledge of environmental codes and regulations. Those with additional training or experience in urban planning increase their opportunities for employment in landscape architecture firms that specialize in site planning as well as landscape design. Many employers prefer to hire entry-level landscape architects who have internship experience, which significantly reduces the amount of on-the-job training required.

TRAINING FOR LANDSCAPE ARCHITECTS

A bachelor's or master's degree in landscape architecture is usually necessary for entry into the profession. The bachelor's degree in landscape architecture takes four or five years to complete.

There are two types of accredited master's degree programs. The master's degree as a first professional degree is a three-year program designed for students with an undergraduate degree in another discipline; this is the most common type. The master's degree as the second professional degree is a two-year program for students who have a bachelor's degree in landscape architecture and wish to teach or specialize in some aspect of landscape architecture, such as regional planning or golf course design.

In 1999, fifty-eight colleges and universities offered seventy-five undergraduate and graduate programs in landscape architecture that were accredited by the Landscape Architecture Accreditation Board of the American Society of Landscape Architects.

College courses required in this field usually include technical subjects such as surveying, landscape design and construction, landscape ecology, site design, and urban and regional planning. Other courses include history of landscape architecture, plant and soil science, geology, professional practice, and general management.

Many landscape architecture programs are adding courses that address environmental issues. In addition, most students at the undergraduate level take a year of prerequisite courses such as English, mathematics, and social and physical science. The design studio is an important aspect of many landscape architecture curriculums. Whenever possible, students are assigned real projects, providing them with valuable hands-on experience. While working on these projects, students become more proficient in the use of computer-aided design, geographic information systems, and video simulation.

In 1999, forty-six states required landscape architects to be licensed or registered. Licensing is based on the Landscape Architect Registration Examination (LARE), sponsored by the Council of Landscape Architectural Registration Boards and administered over a three-day period. Admission to the exam usually requires a degree from an accredited school plus one to four years of work experience, although standards vary from state to state.

Currently, seventeen states require the passage of a state examination in addition to the LARE to satisfy registration requirements. State examinations, which are usually one hour in length and completed at the end of the LARE, focus on laws, environmental regulations, plants, soils, climate, and any other characteristics unique to the state.

Because state requirements for licensure are not uniform, landscape architects may not find it easy to transfer their registration from one state to another. However, those who meet the national standards of graduating from an accredited program, serving three years of internship under the supervision of a registered landscape architect, and passing the LARE can satisfy requirements in most states. Through this means, a landscape architect can obtain certification from the Council of Landscape Architectural Registration Boards, and so gain reciprocity in other states.

In the federal government, candidates for entry positions should have a bachelor's or master's degree in landscape architecture. Unlike state requirements, the federal government does not require its landscape architects to be licensed.

SKILLS NEEDED FOR LANDSCAPE ARCHITECTURE

People planning a career in landscape architecture should appreciate nature, enjoy working with their hands, and possess strong analytical skills. Creative vision and artistic talent are also desirable qualities. Good oral communication skills are essential; landscape architects must be able to convey their ideas to other professionals and clients and to make presentations before large groups. Strong writing skills are also valuable, as is knowledge of computer applications of all kinds, including word processing, desktop publishing, and spreadsheets. Landscape architects will use all these tools to develop presentations, proposals, reports, and land impact studies for clients, colleagues, and superiors. In addition, the ability to draft and design using CAD software is essential.

Many employers recommend that prospective landscape architects complete at least one summer internship with a landscape architecture firm to gain an understanding of the day-to-day operations of a small business, including how to win clients, generate fees, and work within a budget. In addition, on a day-to-day basis, a landscape architect may have to:

- Be attentive to client needs and take responsibility for timely, effective responses.

- Be multi-task oriented; capable of coordinating a variety of projects at one time.

- Be willing and capable of participating in making public presentations.

- Have an understanding of municipal entitlement processes.

- Have good verbal, written, and graphic communication skills.

- Have a working knowledge of AutoCAD 2000, MS Word, and Excel applications.

INTERN LANDSCAPE ARCHITECTS

In states where licensure is required, new hires may be called "apprentices" or "intern landscape architects" until they become licensed. Their duties vary depending on the type and size of employing firm. They may do project research or prepare working drawings, construction documents, or base maps of the area to be landscaped. Some are allowed to participate in the actual design of a project. However, interns must perform all work under the supervision of a licensed landscape architect.

Additionally, all drawings and specifications must be signed and sealed by the licensed landscape architect, who takes legal responsibility for the work. After gaining experience and becoming licensed, landscape architects usually can carry a design through all stages of development. After several years, they may become project managers, taking on the responsibility for meeting schedules and budgets, in addition to overseeing the project design; and later, associates or partners, with a proprietary interest in the business.

SELF-EMPLOYMENT

Many landscape architects are self-employed because start-up costs, after an initial investment in CAD software, are relatively low. Self-discipline, business acumen, and good marketing skills are important qualities for those who choose to open their own business. Even with these qualities, however, some may struggle while building a client base and reputation in the community.

RELATED FIELDS

Those with landscape architecture training also qualify for jobs closely related to landscape architecture, and may, after gaining some experience, become construction supervisors, land or environmental planners, or landscape consultants. Landscape architects use their knowledge of design, construction, land-use planning, and environmental issues to develop a landscape project. Others whose work requires similar skills are architects, surveyors, civil engineers, soil conservationists, and urban and regional planners. Landscape architects also know how to grow and use plants in the landscape. Botanists, who study plants in general, and horticulturists, who study ornamental plants as well as fruit, vegetable, greenhouse, and nursery crops, do similar work.

Landscape Design

A landscape designer works similarly to a landscape architect, but usually on residential or small commercial projects. Landscape designers are not technically certified, therefore, they cannot call themselves landscape architects. For those who do not wish to invest the number of years it takes to become a landscape architect, a career in landscape design could be the answer. You can become a landscape designer after completing a two-year associate's degree in a landscape specialist program offered at a number of schools throughout the country. You should keep in mind that salaries are generally less for designers than architects. On the upside, those who are self-employed are not as limited as those employed by a landscape architecture firm.

Work in landscape design is available almost anywhere you see a tree, a shrub, or a lawn. Job seekers don't have to scour help wanted ads or move across the country to find employment (although doing so could help broaden the scope). Just look around you at all the possibilities. Each of these settings requires a range of workers:

Arboreta	Historic areas	Private homes
Athletic fields	Hospitals	Public parks and gardens
Botanical gardens	Hotels	Recreational facilities
Cemeteries	Museums	Shopping malls
Golf courses	Office buildings	Theme parks
Highways	Playgrounds	University campuses

Historic Landscape Preservation and Landscape Archaeology

Historic landscape preservation is a field of growing interest throughout the country among managers of historic buildings and cultural and natural landscapes. The Colonial Williamsburg Foundation in Williamsburg, Virginia, is one of the largest employers of landscape architects, designers, and related groundskeeping professionals.

Landscape archeology is a fairly new discipline. The purpose is to recover enough evidence to recreate a garden that existed on the site in a given historical period. Landscape archaeology uses traditional archaeological technique to recover the fence lines, planting beds, and other evidence.

Just as with gardening history, there is no particular university degree at this time in landscape archaeology. To become a landscape archaeologist you would have to follow a traditional program in anthropology and archaeology. Then, once you graduated and started getting on-the-job experience, you could specialize. For more information on historic landscape preservation and landscape archaeology, see Kent Brinkley's firsthand account later in this chapter.

Interiorscaping

An interiorscaper works with clients who want to create indoor environments filled with plants. The interiorscaper provides the design, oversees the installation and, if the contract specifies, maintains the health and attractiveness of the layout. Interiorscapers find work with large landscape contracting firms, with nurseries, or they can go it independently, renting space with adequate lighting in a warehouse where they can store their plants. In addition, some large land developers, rather than contracting the work out, hire permanent on-staff interiorscapers to take care of the malls or other complexes they own. Although private homeowners might utilize the services of an interiorscaper, most clients come from the commercial world.

Within the field of interiorscaping there are several different job titles. There are designers, estimators, and operations managers. Interiorscapers utilize the services of installers, delivery people, and job installation supervisors. Maintenance technicians take care of the plants, and maintenance foremen supervise the technicians. Nurseries that employ interiorscapers hire competent sales staff to deal with customers.

The chance for advancement is very good within the industry. With some experience under their belts, installers and maintenance technicians, for example, can move up to supervisory positions or into sales. Many people start out already established in the floral business, as florists or floral designers, for example, and interiorscaping then follows, becoming a natural extension of what they're already doing. A flower shop owner, for example, might stock tropical houseplants for retail. Through walk-in customers from local office buildings, the florist could be requested to add installation and maintenance services.

Entry-level crew workers and technicians can start anywhere from $6 to $13 or $14 an hour. Someone with a new bachelor's degree could expect to earn in the teens or 20s, depending on the region of the country. Designers and managers earn anywhere from $30,000 to $60,000 per year. (See Chapters 7 through 9 for coverage of additional fields related to architecture and landscape architecture.)

JOB HUNTING

With the Internet, job hunting has been made much easier. You are no longer restricted to your own hometown paper or trekking to the library to dig out the Yellow Pages for other regions. A search on the Web will produce dozens, maybe hundreds, of hits. A visit to www.asla.org, the official website of the American Society of Landscape Architects, will bring you to an actual database of current job listings.

SAMPLE JOB LISTINGS

These listings are provided as a sample only and as such, the hiring firms are not mentioned. You may find similar listings by visiting www.asla.org.

Entry-Level Landscape Architect, Arizona

A small, well-established landscape architecture firm is looking for someone with the qualities of a self-starter (motivated, goal-oriented, responsible) who is a quick learner. The ability to work well on his or her own and with a team is a must. The right individual will be proficient in AutoCAD (we have Release 14) and will have the drafting abilities required for occasional hand-drawn items. Knowledge of Southwest plants and quick, high-quality rendering abilities are also a plus. We provide a casual business atmosphere. A full benefits package is provided and flex hour options are available. Our projects cover a wide range, but most are commercial and multifamily projects.

Experience required: none to two years.

Education requirements: B.L.A. or equivalent from an accredited university.

Landscape Architect, Louisiana

We're in search of a motivated self-starter, excited about learning and working the craft of landscape architecture. Our projects vary in scope, scale, and clientele; all are site/construction oriented and premised on advancing technical expertise, design excellence, and construction craftsmanship. This is a small, custom-design studio, not a production sweatshop, and our studio extends to the construction site. We like muddy boots, plants, current technology, and old-fashioned nuts-and-bolts know-how. If you're looking for a traditional, craft-based landscape architecture opportunity, and can demonstrate excellent examples of your own dedication and focus, please contact us for a meeting.

Experience required: one to three years.

Education requirements: Landscape Architect: B.L.A./M.L.A., or others with appropriate supporting skills; horticultural knowledge; strong design skills; construction experience; AutoCAD 14/2000 design and production skills; project management; a rounded perspective on life.

Landscape Architect Assistant, Louisiana

We're in need of an ambitious, mature, design-oriented self-starter who is working toward becoming a career professional. Duties involve participation in all aspects of project management, design, and CAD-based drafting production; office operations; limited field-related activities. This is a wide-open opportunity to learn by doing, assist project designers, meet clients, work in a small, creative studio environment, and participate in on-site design and construction-phase activities. This position demands self-discipline, motivation, and teamwork. In addition to professional-related activities, general office assistance regarding daily business operations is included. All work will be preformed under the immediate supervision of a registered landscape architect.

Experience required: None.

Education requirements: Bachelor's degree; award from recognized certificate program in landscape architecture, architecture, or complimentary discipline; AutoCAD and other computer experience preferred.

Green Space Designer, Utah

Green Space Design is a new idea and landscape architecture realm developed by an award-winning firm focused on preserving landscapes. Green Space Design designs open space into community plans, connecting critical lands into one system. The process defines open space types, utilizes GIS and satellite imagery to map them, calls on public participation to identify and design a green space vision, and implements that vision through a spectrum of planning and preservation tools. Green space is created commensurate with growth, building a green infrastructure that balances preservation and development economically and equitably.

This is a project manager position within a three-person core of land designers, involving interviews/meetings/presentations with community members; landscape analysis/mapping; and updating planning documents. Superior written, verbal, and graphic communication; a commitment to marketing projects; moderate computer skills (desktop publishing, GIS, CAD); a comprehensive understanding of land and natural systems; and ability to travel the Intermountain Region are essential. The ideal candidate should be versed and vocal in land conservation, smart growth, and public participation in planning.

Experience required: three years desired, but enthusiasm and interest weigh heavily.

Education requirements: B.L.A. or M.L.A.

Landscape Architect Extraordinaire, Vermont

A firm of 300-plus planners, engineers, landscape architects, and scientists is looking for a landscape architect (guru) to lead and manage its Landscape Architecture and Planning Group. You will be working with a staff of talented and motivated landscape architects and planners, coordinating with our fifteen offices in the Northeast, Southeast, and Southwest. You must be an innovator, mentor, doer-seller, with a whatever-it-takes attitude. If you are ready to live in a gorgeous place, work hard for a company that offers great pay and benefits, and make a mark in the profession, send in your resume and portfolio.

Experience required: twenty-plus years of diverse design and leadership.

Education requirements: Minimum B.L.A.

SALARIES FOR LANDSCAPE ARCHITECTS

In 1998 median annual earnings for landscape architects were $37,930. The middle 50 percent earned between $28,820 and $50,550. The lowest 10 percent earned less than $22,800, and the highest 10 percent earned over $78,920. Most landscape architects worked in the landscape and horticultural services industry, where median annual earnings were $33,600 in 1997 (the most recent figures available). In 1999 the average annual salary for all landscape architects in the federal government in nonsupervisory, supervisory, and managerial positions was about $57,500.

Because many landscape architects work for small firms or are self-employed, benefits tend to be less generous than those provided to workers in large organizations.

FIRSTHAND ACCOUNTS

Kent Brinkley, Landscape Architect

Kent Brinkley is a landscape architect and garden historian at Colonial Williamsburg. He has a B.A in history from Mary Baldwin College in Staunton, Virginia. He has been with the Colonial Williamsburg Foundation for more than ten years.

Getting Started

"I came to landscape architecture through the back door. I started as a draftsman and worked my way up to vice president of the firm before coming to my current position here at Colonial Williamsburg Foundation. When I got my job here I was ecstatic. This was the perfect marriage of my love of history and my work as a landscape architect. It's been wonderful to be able to take two major interests and combine them in a way that allows me to do both."

What the Work Is Like

"I wear a lot of different hats. I sit at a drawing board and I create designs for new work that's taking place. We also have many gardens that were designed during the 1930s and '40s by my predecessors. They conducted extensive research and chose plants that were known and used in the eighteenth century.

But in a few cases, a plant they chose, even though it was appropriate to the period, might not flourish in a specific location because of too much sunlight or too much shade. So we try to come up with something else that would have been used but will grow better in that specific location.

"Many of these gardens are forty or fifty years old and, unlike the architecture where you just replace fabric when a board rots or you're putting a coat of paint on, plant materials do grow. They're dynamic, and when you have a garden that's mature, or overmature as many of ours happen to be, part of my charge is looking at the replacements that inevitably have to be factored in when plants or trees die out. This keeps it looking presentable to the public.

"I work closely with the person responsible for the maintenance. I provide the design expertise and we talk about what is needed in a particular garden. Once a decision has been made, he directs his maintenance staff to implement the work.

"I also spend time giving slide lectures to groups and garden clubs. I give garden tours a couple of times a month to the public just to have contact with the visitors on the street.

"I'm also a garden historian. That is someone who has a background in history and has done research and is interested in the development of the historical landscape over time. I've made any number of trips to England in the last fourteen or fifteen years and have visited many country estates and gardens over there. I've looked at English landscape design, which served as the precedent for many of the designs in the eighteenth century here in the Virginia Colony. Much of my work involves looking at what was done historically in gardens. The kinds of plants that were grown, how they were laid out, the types of fencing they were using—it's all part of knowing how to recreate a period garden.

"It's a specialty someone comes to within a history curriculum. It's a young field in this country; it didn't start as a discipline until 1975. If this interests you, you would combine history courses with horticulture courses. Of course, the job market is fairly small, but it's growing. Right now most jobs are at living history museums such as Williamsburg, or Sturbridge Village and Plimoth Plantation in Massachusetts.

"Here we have colonial gardens that have been recreated, duplicating the plants used during the eighteenth century. And beautiful three- and four-hundred-year-old trees still stand, lining the hard-packed dirt walkways. All of this restoration work was accomplished only after extensive archaeological and historical investigation.

"Part of my job is to work in concert with archaeologists when they're doing excavations on a particular site. A few years ago, for example, a summer field school from the College of William and Mary was in progress. We excavated a garden in town. This particular site was the home of Saint George Tucker, a fairly prominent Virginian in the eighteenth century whose papers have survived. We know a good bit about his interest in gardening and the things he was growing, so it was very exciting to see what the archaeology turned up, finding physical evidence of his garden—evidence of pathways, fence lines and postholes—they leave a definite dark stain. We can also find planting beds and out-building foundations, brick foundations of dairies and chicken coops.

"When you excavate the soil from the planting bed, you sometimes find seed materials in the soil samples. You screen the soil and take it into a lab. There's a method known as flotation, which separates the water from the soil, and any minute particles and seeds can be recovered. Then using a microscope you can identify the type of plant from the seed. We can also do pollen analysis. But it's problematical because you don't always know how the seeds ended up in the bed. They could have been dropped by birds or blown by wind.

"We can solve that particular problem with phytolith analysis. Phytolith analysis looks at the mineralized tissues of plants. A plant absorbs water and minerals through its root system. When a plant dies the liquid material will crystallize, and when it does, it takes on an impression of the plant cell wall structure. Then all the phytoliths are deposited in the soil as the plant decays. Unlike seeds or pollen, which could have gotten there for a number of reasons, when you find phytolith in the soil sample, you can be 99 percent certain the plant was actually grown there and didn't just happen."

Advice from Kent Brinkley

"People who are mechanically inclined or are curious how things fit together and work would probably find landscape architecture and drafting to their liking. There is a lot of drafting involved; you have to know how to cultivate that drawing talent.

"You also have to have good English skills. You need the ability to write and speak well because you're working with people every day. You might have to get up in front of a group and make a presentation to sell your designs. Some sales ability is a good thing to have; you have to market yourself, your firm, and the design, and be able to persuade people that this is the way to go. You can never waste your time by taking additional English or drawing courses.

"Once you've graduated, you should work in several different offices and gain different kinds of experiences for the first five or six years. It's not a good idea to lock yourself into any one place. I would also recommend that you work in the field for two or three years before taking the licensing exam. It's comprehensive in scope and tests you on a variety of things. You need to get some experience under your belt before you try to tackle it.

"I think there's a bright future for people in this field in the twenty-first century because we are the ones who have a broad enough range of expertise to consider environmental concerns in addition to aesthetics in order to make the resulting projects user-friendly and earth-friendly."

Greg Blackwell, Landscape Architect/Interiorscaper

Greg Blackwell works for Creative Plantings, a large contracting firm in Burtonsville, Maryland. He is a registered landscape architect with a strong interest in interior design. He started with a B.S. in horticulture from Virginia, specializing in landscape design.

Most interiorscaping programs fall under the auspices of a landscape architecture or landscape design program. Community colleges also offer courses, but a degree is not necessary to pursue a career as an interiorscaper; many firms will take on interns and provide on-the-job training.

What the Work Is Like

"My firm works with hotels, office buildings, shopping malls, restaurants, corporate headquarters, and other types of both large and small businesses. On any given project, we first meet with clients to discuss their needs and what they're looking for, from a planting and design standpoint, that will also be within their budget. In the initial visit, I try to get as much information as I can to work with, including blueprints of the buildings, light readings, colors and accents in the surroundings, types of finishes and furniture styles, and sources of water. In larger jobs, the time of year might be important. For example, because of freezing temperatures, you may have to protect material from the cold weather during the delivery process.

"Then, if it's possible, we like our clients to visit our facility. We have greenhouses where they can pick out particular plants. We also have photographs we can show them. Depending on the person, the client might want to leave it all up to you or stay involved throughout the process.

"Next, I'll write up specifications, including detailed drawings and layout, and artist renderings, to show what the space would look like with plants, and the different kinds of containers and finishes. After I work on the plans and have my presentation prepared, I meet with the clients again and present my ideas to them. If they approve the plan, the next step would be organizing and obtaining the materials. If we don't have them in stock, then I will go directly to the growers, wholesalers, or importers in Florida, select the materials, and tag the plants I'll need.

"We then schedule delivery and installation and coordinate with the other trades. Interiorscapers are usually the last people in on a project, especially if it's a new building, because we have to wait until all the construction is done.

"After the job is installed, we usually come back on a weekly basis to clean the plants and inspect them for any insects or disease. If there is a situation in which sunlight is coming in strongly from one side, we have to rotate the plants because they start facing toward the sun. And we'll also replace any plants that aren't doing well.

"In addition, I am responsible for estimating, inventory, purchasing, and photography. I use photography to chronicle possible plant arrangements for customers and also to enter designs into professional competitions.

"Clients of Creative Plantings have two choices: they can either purchase the plants and containers outright and have a separate monthly maintenance contract, or they can lease the entire package for one monthly payment and a small up-front charge.

"We also provide short-term rentals for conventions, weddings, and other types of special events, including large-scale events such as the inauguration and all the balls here in Washington, D.C."

**Advice from
Greg Blackwell**

"I would encourage you to consider self-employment. While interiorscapers with large firms or nurseries usually have a selection of plants already in stock, a self-employed designer could operate with only a small inventory. It is possible, utilizing pictures, to set up a job with a client, and then order the plants needed from a local wholesaler. This way, you can run a lucrative business with relatively low overhead costs."

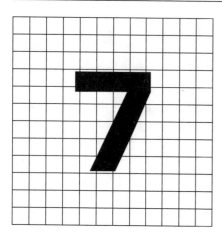

ENGINEERING

The design of buildings often requires the special expertise of civil, structural, architectural, mechanical, and electrical engineers. Engineers have many options and are in considerable demand from the industry—from corporate clients and manufacturers of building products—and private practice. Engineers offering design services for building projects typically practice as independent consultants in one of the areas listed or as a specialty engineer (for example, acoustical, illumination, or fire protection). Some engineering firms combine two or more of these areas. For example, some may offer a combination of architecture, construction management, or design-build services.

ENGINEERING SPECIALIZATIONS

There are many possible areas of specialization for those interested in the field of engineering, and each one is integral to the building and construction of a variety of projects. The major areas of specialization in engineering are civil, structural, architectural, mechanical, and electrical and electronics engineering.

Civil engineers. Civil engineers specialize in the design, construction, and operation of facilities essential to modern life. These include building, highways, airport, pipelines, bridges, dams, irrigation systems, drainage systems, water-supply and distribution systems, and wastewater treatment works.

Structural engineers. Structural engineers specialize in the design of bridges, buildings, telecommunications towers, dams, space platforms, amusement park rides, and more, with attention to the ability to withstand forces or "loads" from people, vehicles, gusting winds, extreme temperatures, pressures of earth and water, earthquakes, and so on. At the undergraduate level, the study of various structural engineering topics is generally part of the course of study leading to the bachelor's degree in civil engineering.

Architectural engineers. Architectural engineers specialize in the analysis, design, construction, and operation of engineered systems for commercial, industrial, and institutional buildings and other facilities. Building systems include electrical, communications and control, lighting, heating, ventilating, air-conditioning, fire protection, plumbing, acoustical, and structural systems.

Mechanical engineers. Mechanical engineers specialize in the research, development, design, manufacture, and testing of tools, engines, machines, and other mechanical devices. They work on power-producing machines such as electricity-producing generators, internal combustion engines, steam and gas turbines, and jet and rocket engines. They also develop power-using machines such as refrigeration and air-conditioning equipment, robots used in manufacturing, machine tools, materials handling systems, and industrial production equipment. Mechanical engineers also design tools needed by other engineers for their work.

Electrical and electronics engineers. Electrical and electronics engineers specialize in different areas such as power generation, transmission, and distribution; communications; computer electronics; and electrical equipment manufacturing, or a subdivision of these areas—industrial robot control systems or aviation electronics, for example. Electrical and electronics engineers design new products, write performance requirements, and develop maintenance schedules. They also test equipment, solve operating problems, and estimate the time and cost of engineering projects.

POSSIBLE EMPLOYERS

Civil, structural, and architectural engineers are employed by government agencies, public utility companies, private consulting firms, construction companies, architectural firms, and universities.

Mechanical engineering is the broadest engineering discipline, extending across many interdependent specialties. Mechanical engineers work in many industries, and their work varies by industry and function.

Electrical and electronics engineering is the largest branch of engineering. Electrical and electronics engineers work for engineering and business consulting firms; government agencies; manufacturers of electrical and electronic equipment, industrial machinery, and professional and scientific instruments; communications and utilities firms; manufacturers of aircraft and guided missiles; and computer and data processing services firms.

TRAINING FOR ENGINEERS

A bachelor's degree in engineering is generally required for entry-level engineering jobs. College graduates with a degree in a physical science or mathematics may occasionally qualify for some engineering jobs, especially in specialties in high demand.

Most engineering degrees are granted in electrical, mechanical, or civil engineering. However, engineers trained in one branch may work in related branches. For example, many aerospace engineers have training in mechanical engineering. This flexibility allows employers to meet staffing needs in new technologies and specialties in which engineers are in short supply. It also allows engineers to shift to fields with better employment prospects or to ones that match their interests more closely.

In addition to the standard engineering degree, many colleges offer degrees in engineering technology, which are offered as either two- or four-year programs. These programs prepare students for practical design and production work, rather than for jobs requiring more theoretical and scientific knowledge. Graduates of four-year technology programs may get jobs similar to those obtained by graduates with a bachelor's degree in engineering. Some employers regard technology program graduates as having skills between those of a technician and an engineer.

Graduate training is essential for engineering faculty positions, but is not required for the majority of entry-level engineering jobs. Many engineers obtain graduate degrees in engineering or business administration to learn new technology, broaden their education, and enhance their promotion opportunities. Many high-level executives in government and industry began their careers as engineers. Sometimes, architects leave the field and retrain for a career in engineering.

About 320 colleges and universities offer bachelor's degree programs in engineering that are accredited by the Accreditation Board for Engineering and Technology (ABET), and about 250 colleges offer accredited bachelor's degree programs in engineering technology. ABET accreditation is based on an examination of an engineering program's student achievement, program improvement, faculty, curricular content, facilities, and institutional commitment. Although most institutions offer programs in the major branches of engineering, only a few offer some of the smaller specialties. Also, programs of the same title may vary in content. For example, some programs emphasize industrial practices, preparing students for a job in industry, whereas others are more theoretical and are better for students preparing to take graduate work. Therefore, students should investigate curricula and check accreditation carefully before selecting a college.

Admissions requirements for undergraduate engineering schools include a solid background in mathematics (algebra, geometry, trigonometry, and calculus), sciences (biology, chemistry, and physics), and courses in English, social studies, humanities, and computers.

Bachelor's degree programs in engineering are typically designed to last four years, but many students find that it takes between four and five years to complete their studies. In a typical four-year college curriculum, the first two years are spent studying mathematics, basic sciences, introductory engineering, humanities, and social sciences. In the last two years, most courses are in engineering, usually with a concentration in one branch. You should also know that some engineering schools and two-year colleges have agreements that the two-year college provide the initial engineering education, and the engineering school automatically admits students for their last two years. In addition, a few engineering schools have arrangements that a student spends three years in a liberal arts college, studying pre-engineering subjects, and two years in an engineering school studying core subjects, and then receives a bachelor's degree from each school.

Research colleges and universities thoroughly to determine if they offer additional educational incentives. For example, some schools offer cooperative plans that combine classroom study and practical work, permitting students to gain valuable experience and finance part of their education.

LICENSURE

All fifty states and the District of Columbia require licensure for engineers whose work may affect life, health, or property, or who offer their services to the public. Engineers who are licensed are called Professional Engineers (PE). This licensure generally requires a degree from an ABET-accredited engineering program, four years of relevant work experience, and successful completion of a state examination. Recent graduates can start the licensing process by taking the examination in two stages. The initial examination can be taken upon graduation. Engineers who pass this examination are commonly called Engineers in Training (EIT). The EIT certification is usually valid for ten years. After acquiring suitable work experience, EITs can take the second examination, the Principles and Practice of Engineering Exam. While Professional Engineers must be licensed in each state in which they practice, most states recognize licensure from other states. Many civil, electrical, mechanical, and chemical engineers are certified as PEs.

GETTING STARTED AND GETTING AHEAD

Engineers should be creative, inquisitive, analytical, and detail-oriented. They should be able to work as part of a team and be able to communicate well, both orally and in writing. If you possess most or all of these skills, you may excel in this diverse field.

Beginning engineering graduates usually work under the supervision of experienced engineers and, in large companies, may also receive formal classroom or seminar-type training. As new engineers gain knowledge and experience, they are assigned more difficult projects with greater independence to develop designs, solve problems, and make decisions. With increasing experience and responsibility, engineers advance to become technical specialists or to supervise a staff or team of engineers and technicians. Some eventually become engineering managers or enter other managerial or sales jobs.

SAMPLE PROGRAM

A search on the Internet or contacting the appropriate professional associations listed in Appendix A will lead you to hundreds of engineering programs. Featured below is a composite program, included to give you an idea of what to expect at the college or university of your choice. As mentioned earlier, programs differ in their emphasis, so it's important to investigate each school thoroughly before making a decision.

Department of Civil and Architectural Engineering

The department of Civil and Architectural Engineering offers two undergraduate degrees accredited by the Engineering Accreditation Commission of the Accreditation Board for Engineering and Technology (ABET):

1. Bachelor of Science in Civil Engineering (B.S.C.E.) and

2. Bachelor of Science in Architectural Engineering (B.S.A.E.)

A Five-Year B.S./M.S. program leads to both the B.S. and M.S. degrees in civil engineering in five years. This program is open to exceptional students who are admitted to the graduate program in their junior year. The Five-Year B.S./M.S. program leads to the following two degrees:

1. B.S./M.S. in Architectural Engineering and

2. B.S./M.S. in Civil Engineering

The department also offers graduate programs leading to the following degrees:

1. Master of Science in Architectural Engineering (M.S.A.E)

2. Master of Science in Civil Engineering

3. Doctor of Philosophy (Ph.D.) in Civil Engineering, and

4. Doctor of Arts (D.A.) in Civil Engineering.

Architectural and Civil Engineering

The goal of the architectural engineering program at the University is to prepare graduates for traditional entry-level positions in the building industry, as well as for graduate programs leading to further specialization in any of the major discipline areas of architectural engineering. The educational objectives of the architectural and civil engineering programs are to produce graduates who: (a) have a sound background in the fundamentals of engineering, and are prepared to practice architectural engineering in the areas of structures, environmental systems, and construction management; (b) have the abilities and education expected by industry; and (c) are prepared to enter graduate or professional degree programs, as well as other careers.

The architectural engineering curriculum provides an integrated educational experience in mathematics, basic sciences, humanities, social sciences, engineering sciences, and architectural engineering design. The architectural engineering program integrates design applications across the curriculum, beginning with materials and methods of construction, and architectural design in the sophomore year, and continuing with structural and building services design in the junior and senior years.

The civil engineering curriculum provides an integrated educational experience in mathematics, basic sciences, humanities, social sciences, engineering sciences, and civil engineering design. The first two years of the civil engineering curriculum are intended to provide a strong foundation in mathematics and basic sciences. During the next two years of the four-year program, the civil engineering curriculum integrates engineering sciences with design applications in the areas of structural, environment, geotechnical, and transportation engineering. The curriculum culminates with a major senior-level design project that includes design applications from the major disciplines of civil engineering.

SALARIES FOR ENGINEERS

Civil/Structural/Architectural Engineers. Median annual earnings of were $53,450 in 1998. The middle 50 percent earned between $41,800 and $74,550. The lowest 10 percent earned less than $34,270, and the highest 10 percent earned more than $87,350.

Median annual earnings in the industries employing the largest numbers of civil, structural, or architectural engineers are

Federal government	$64,000
Heavy construction, except highway	$61,300
Local government, except education and hospitals	$52,100
Engineering and architectural services	$49,300
State government, except education and hospitals	$48,900

According to a 1999 salary survey by the National Association of Colleges and Employers, bachelor's degree candidates in civil engineering received starting offers averaging about $36,100 a year; master's degree candidates in civil engineering, $42,300; and Ph.D. candidates in civil engineering, $58,600.

Mechanical engineers. Median annual earnings of mechanical engineers were $53,290 in 1998. The middle 50 percent earned between $42,680 and $74,220. The lowest 10 percent earned less than $35,290, and the highest 10 percent earned more than $87,000.

Median annual earnings in the industries employing the largest numbers of mechanical engineers are

Federal government	$66,800
Engineering and architectural services	$55,800
Electronic components and accessories	$52,900
Aircraft and parts	$51,800
Motor vehicles and equipment	$48,500

According to a 1999 salary survey by the National Association of Colleges and Employers, bachelor's degree candidates in mechanical engineering received starting offers averaging about $43,300 a year; master's degree candidates, $51,900; and Ph.D. candidates, $64,300.

Electrical and electronics engineers. Median annual earnings of electrical and electronics engineers were $62,660 in 1998. The middle 50 percent earned between $47,080 and $80,160. The lowest 10 percent earned less than $38,470, and the highest 10 percent earned more than $91,490.

Median annual earnings in the industries employing the largest numbers of electrical and electronics engineers are

Federal government	$68,000
Computer and office equipment	$67,100
Electronic components and accessories	$59,900
Communications equipment	$59,400
Engineering and architectural services	$58,900

According to a 1999 salary survey by the National Association of Colleges and Employers, bachelor's degree candidates in electrical and electronics engineering received starting offers averaging about $45,200 a year; master's degree candidates, $57,200; and Ph.D. candidates, $70,800.

JOB OUTLOOK

According to the U.S. Bureau of Labor Statistics, employment opportunities in engineering are expected to be good through the year 2008. Overall engineering employment is expected to increase about as fast as the average for all occupations, while the number of engineering degrees granted has remained fairly constant over the past several years.

Projected growth varies by specialty, ranging from a decline among mining engineers to faster-than-average growth among electrical and electronics engineers. Competitive pressures and advancing technology will force companies to improve and update product designs increasingly more frequently, and to optimize their manufacturing processes.

Employers will rely on engineers to increase productivity further, as investment in plant and equipment increases to expand output of goods and services. New computer systems have improved the design process, enabling engineers to produce and analyze various product designs much more rapidly than in the past. Despite these widespread applications, computer technology is not expected to limit employment opportunities.

Finally, additional engineers will be needed to improve or build new roads, bridges, water and pollution control systems, and other public facilities.

Many engineering jobs are related to developing technologies used in national defense. Because defense expenditures—particularly expenditures for aircraft, missiles, and other weapons systems—are not expected to return to previously high levels, job outlook may not be as favorable for engineers working in defense-related fields.

The number of bachelor's degrees awarded in engineering began declining in 1987, and continued to stay at about the same level through much of the 1990s. Although it is difficult to project engineering enrollments, the total number of graduates from engineering programs is not expected to increase significantly over the projection period. Some engineering schools have restricted enrollments, especially in defense-related fields, such as aerospace engineering, to accommodate reduced job opportunities.

Although only a relatively small proportion of engineers leaves the profession each year, many job openings will arise from replacement needs. A greater proportion of replacement openings is created by engineers who transfer to management, sales, or other professional specialty occupations than by those who leave the labor force.

Most industries are less likely to lay off engineers than other workers. Many engineers work on long-term research and development projects or in other activities that continue even during economic slowdowns. In industries such as electronics and aerospace, however, large cutbacks in defense expenditures and government research and development funds, as well as the trend toward contracting out engineering work to engineering services firms, have resulted in significant layoffs for engineers.

CONTINUING EDUCATION FOR ENGINEERS

It is important for engineers, like those working in other technical occupations, to continue their education throughout their careers, because much of their value to their employer depends on their knowledge of the latest technology. Although the pace of technological change varies by engineering specialty and industry, advances in technology have affected every engineering discipline significantly. Engineers in high-technology areas, such as advanced electronics, may find that technical knowledge can become obsolete rapidly. Even those who continue their education are vulnerable if the particular technology or product in which they have specialized becomes obsolete. By keeping current in their field, engineers are able to deliver the best solutions and greatest value to their employers. Engineers who have not kept current in their field may find themselves passed over for promotions or vulnerable to layoffs, should they occur. On the other hand, it is often these high-technology areas that offer the greatest challenges, the most interesting work, and the highest salaries. Therefore, the choice of engineering specialty and employer involves an assessment not only of the potential rewards but also of the risk of technological obsolescence.

SAMPLE JOB LISTINGS

These listings are provided as a sample only and as such, the hiring firms are not mentioned. You may find similar listings by doing an Internet search using keywords such as "jobs" and "engineering."

Architectural Engineer, Arizona

A firm active in national and international markets for over fifty-four years has a position for a Registered Architect/Project Manager. Candidate must be a team player with design talent, leadership skills, and approximately ten years of experience in the health-care or educational field. Registration and AutoCAD experience required.

Structural Manager, Colorado

Opportunity for skilled and ambitious engineer. We need motivated, creative self-starters for the structural manager position. Management of staff and ownership opportunity. PE or the ability to become licensed within one year desirable. Experienced wood frame designer, some steel and concrete, for residential and small commercial projects. Experience with design in snow country helpful. This is a very challenging position to work with architectural masterpieces. Seven to ten years' experience. Flexible hours, excellent benefits, and top salary. We are a small ten-person office.

Civil/Site Design Engineer, Iowa

One of the top engineering and architectural firms in the country is looking for energetic and creative engineers. As a project engineer, you will be responsible for site design, planning, and development, as well as roadway, drainage, utilities, and grading. A B.S.C.E. and three to five-plus years' experience required. EIT/PE preferred, as is InRoads and Microstation experience.

Electrical Engineer/PE, Vermont

Must have PE license. Experience in design of LV, MV, and HV power systems. Work includes relaying theory and application, short circuit analysis, load flow analysis.

B.S.M.E.-EIT/PE preferred, not mandatory with five-plus years' experience in design of HVAC, plumbing, and fire protection systems. Commercial and institutional buildings with emphasis on hospital and critical facilities.

FIRSTHAND ACCOUNT

Maggie Shannon Wagenaar, Civil Engineer

Maggie Shannon Wagenaar is the president of her South Florida company, Sunbelt Environmental, which she formed in 1986. She is a registered professional engineer with a bachelor's degree in civil engineering from Virginia Polytechnic Institute and State University.

Getting Started

"I attended Virginia Polytechnic Institute and State University and earned my B.S. in civil engineering technology in 1976. Not surprisingly, I was the only woman in my program, and because of that, I felt isolated at times. The men would get together and study in their dorms or fraternity houses, but I lived at home and had to work alone. And since I was the only woman, I stuck out like a sore thumb. I could never skip a class or slack off—everyone would notice. As a result, I was forced to learn more on my own, become more independent. But I had the support of my professors, and that helped a lot.

"I worked in one department where I was the only registered PE. I put in longer hours than anyone else, I always took work home with me, and yet my salary was the lowest. I could have gone to court dozens of times.

"Discrimination is a way of life for women in this field, especially younger women, but I've seen some women commit professional suicide by pursuing it. If you dwell on it, make a huge issue of it, you can end up being blackballed. Yes, it hurts sometimes, but I think the best course is to ignore it—and work as hard as you can to prove them wrong.

"After I graduated, I continued with my plan of hard work. Putting in sixty- to eighty-hour weeks for the next ten years, I moved up from junior engineer and project engineer to project manager. And in 1986, I opened my own firm."

What the Work Is Like

"When you're the boss, you call the shots and you don't have to worry about other distracting issues. I am able to devote my energy to my number one interest, preserving the environment. My main goal is to help keep this world livable, and water purity is one cause with which I'm particularly concerned. It's a precious commodity, and though there are many good laws and regulations to force us to pay attention, many still don't see how precious water really is.

"Sunbelt Environmental is a small firm with anywhere from six to ten employees, depending on current workload. It's my intention to keep it small because it's my feeling that if a company gets too large, then the president ends up spending more time on employee matters than on the outside world. With computer technology—and we utilize all the latest—a small firm can accomplish a lot.

"Running a business is far more demanding than I had realized when I first started out. It has its ups and downs but it's always challenging and I love it."

Advice from Maggie Shannon Wagenaar

"If you're just starting out, and you're a woman, it might help to know that it does get easier as you get older. If you work hard over the years to build a proven track record, one that no one can dispute, meet your deadlines, and show that you have a firm commitment, it really does help to change attitudes. Clients and colleagues will, more often than not, notice your capabilities and not your gender."

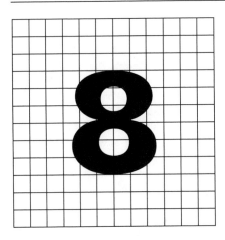

URBAN AND REGIONAL PLANNING

Historically, urban planning has been closely associated with architecture. Increasingly, however, planning is concerned with economics, demographics, and public policy as well as land use and community development. Planners perform a variety of tasks, from transportation studies to environmental-impact assessments and zoning-code analyses.

A few independent planning firms exist, but most planners are employed by larger architecture and engineering firms or at various levels of state and local government. Many architecture schools offer degree programs in planning, usually at the master's and doctoral levels.

DUTIES

Planners develop long- and short-term land use plans to provide for growth and revitalization of urban, suburban, and rural communities, while helping local officials make decisions concerning social, economic, and environmental problems. Because local governments employ the majority of urban and regional planners, they are often referred to as community, regional, or city planners. Planners also promote the best use of a community's land and resources for residential, commercial, institutional, and recreational purposes. Planners may be involved in various other activities, including decisions on alternative public transportation system plans, resource development, and protection of ecologically sensitive regions. They address issues such as traffic congestion, air pollution, and the effect of growth and change on a community. They may formulate plans relating to the construction of school buildings, public housing, or other infrastructures. Some planners are involved in environmental issues ranging from pollution control to wetland preservation, forest conservation, or the location of new landfills. Planners also may be involved with drafting legislation on environmental, social, and economic issues, such as sheltering the homeless, planning a new park, or meeting the demand for new correctional facilities.

Planners examine proposed community facilities such as schools to be sure these facilities will meet the changing demands placed upon them over time. They keep abreast of economic and legal issues involved in zoning codes, building codes, and environmental regulations. They ensure that builders and developers follow these codes and regulations. Planners also deal with land use issues created by population movements. For example, as suburban growth and economic development create more new jobs outside cities, the need for public transportation that enables workers to get to these jobs increases. In response, planners develop transportation models for possible implementation and explain their details to planning boards and the general public.

Before preparing plans for community development, planners report on the current use of land for residential, business, and community purposes. These reports include information on the location and capacity of streets, highways, water and sewer lines, schools, libraries, and cultural and recreational sites. They also provide data on the types of industries in the community, characteristics of the population, and employment and economic trends. With this information, along with input from citizens' advisory committees, planners design the layout of land uses for buildings and other facilities such as subway lines and stations, and prepare reports showing how their programs can be carried out and what they will cost.

Planners use computers to record and analyze information, and to prepare reports and recommendations for government executives and others. Computer databases, spreadsheets, and analytical techniques are widely used to project program costs and forecast future trends in employment, housing, transportation, or population. Computerized geographic information systems enable planners to map land areas and overlay maps with geographic variables, such as population density, as well as to combine and manipulate geographic information to produce alternative plans for land use or development.

Urban and regional planners often confer with land developers, civic leaders, and public officials. They may function as mediators in community disputes and present alternatives acceptable to opposing parties. Planners may prepare material for community relations programs, speak at civic meetings, and appear before legislative committees and elected officials to explain and defend their proposals.

In large organizations, planners usually specialize in a single area such as transportation, demography, housing, historic preservation, urban design, environmental and regulatory issues, or economic development. In small organizations, planners must be able to do various kinds of planning.

WORKING CONDITIONS FOR PLANNERS

Urban and regional planners are often required to travel to inspect the features of land under consideration for development or regulation, including its current use and the types of structures on it. Some local government planners involved in site development inspections spend most of their time in the field. Although most planners have a scheduled forty-hour workweek, they frequently attend evening or weekend meetings or public hearings with citizens' groups. Planners may experience the pressure of deadlines and tight work schedules, as well as political pressure generated by interest groups affected by land use proposals.

EMPLOYMENT FIGURES

Urban and regional planners hold about 35,000 jobs nationwide, and about six out of ten are employed by local governments. An increasing proportion of planners is employed in the private sector for companies involved with research and testing or management and public relations. Others are employed in state agencies dealing with housing, transportation, or environmental protection, and a small number work for the federal government.

JOB OUTLOOK

According to the Bureau of Labor Statistics, employment of urban and regional planners is expected to grow about as fast as the average for all occupations through 2008. This growth is a result of the need for state and local governments to provide public services such as regulation of commercial development, the environment, transportation, housing, and land use and development. Nongovernmental initiatives dealing with historic preservation and redevelopment will provide additional openings. Some job openings will also arise from the need to replace experienced planners who transfer to other occupations, retire, or leave the labor force for other reasons.

Most planners work for local governments with limited resources and many demands for services. When communities need to cut expenditures, planning services may be cut before more basic services such as police or education. As a result, the number of openings in private industry for consulting positions is expected to grow more rapidly than the number of openings in government.

Most new jobs for urban and regional planners will arise in more affluent, rapidly expanding communities. Local governments need planners to address an array of problems associated with population growth. For example, new housing developments require roads, sewer systems, fire stations, schools, libraries, and recreation facilities that must be planned while considering budgetary constraints. Small town chambers of commerce, economic development authorities, and tourism bureaus may hire planners, preferring candidates with some background in marketing and public relations.

TRAINING FOR PLANNERS

Employers prefer workers who have advanced training. Most entry-level jobs in federal, state, and local government agencies require a master's degree in urban or regional planning, urban design, geography, or a similar course of study. For some positions, a bachelor's degree and related work experience is sufficient. A bachelor's degree from an accredited planning program, coupled with a master's degree in architecture, landscape architecture, or civil engineering, is good preparation for entry-level planning jobs in areas such as urban design, transportation, or the environment.

A master's degree from an accredited planning program provides the best training for a number of planning fields. Although graduates from one of the limited number of accredited bachelor's degree programs qualify for many entry-level positions, their advancement opportunities are often limited unless they acquire an advanced degree.

Courses in related disciplines such as architecture, law, earth sciences, demography, economics, finance, health administration, geographic information systems, and management are highly recommended. In addition, familiarity with computer models and statistical techniques is necessary.

In 1999 about eighty colleges and universities offered an accredited master's degree program, and about ten offered an accredited bachelor's degree program in urban or regional planning. These programs are accredited by the Planning Accreditation Board, which consists of representatives of the American Institute of Certified Planners, the American Planning Association, and the Association of Collegiate Schools of Planning. Most graduate programs in planning require a minimum of two years. Specialized courses most commonly offered by planning schools are environmental planning, land use and comprehensive planning, economic development, housing, historic preservation, and social planning. Other popular offerings include community development, transportation, and urban design.

Graduate students spend considerable time in studios, workshops, and laboratory courses learning to analyze and solve planning problems. They are often required to work in a planning office part-time or during the summer. Local government planning offices frequently offer students internships, providing experience that proves invaluable in obtaining a full-time planning position after graduation.

The American Institute of Certified Planners (AICP), a professional institute within the American Planning Association (APA), grants certification to individuals who have the appropriate combination of education and professional experience and pass an examination. Certification may be helpful for promotion.

Planners must be able to think in terms of spatial relationships and visualize the effects of their plans and designs. Planners should be flexible and able to reconcile different viewpoints and to make constructive policy recommendations. The ability to communicate effectively, both orally and in writing, is necessary for anyone interested in this field.

After a few years of experience, planners may advance to assignments requiring a high degree of independent judgment, such as designing the physical layout of a large development or recommending policy and budget options. Some public sector planners are promoted to community planning director and spend a great deal of time meeting with officials, speaking to civic groups, and supervising a staff. Further advancement occurs through a transfer to a larger jurisdiction with more complex problems and greater responsibilities, or into related occupations, such as director of community or economic development.

SALARIES

Median annual earnings of urban and regional planners are about $42,860. The middle 50 percent earn between $32,920 and $56,150 a year. The lowest 10 percent earn less than $26,020, and the highest 10 percent earn more than $80,090 a year. Median annual earnings for urban and regional planners last year were $40,700 in local government and $38,900 in state government.

SAMPLE JOB LISTINGS

These listings are provided as a sample only and as such, the hiring firms are not mentioned. You may find similar listings by visiting www.asla.org.

Urban Designer/Illustrator, Nevada

A major city is seeking an experienced professional to serve in the capacity of Urban Designer/Illustrator with a city growth program. This position will work closely with Design Officer in visually communicating the application of our growth initiative through three-dimensional, computer-simulated illustrations in the following arenas of urban design:

- Infill and redevelopment ordinance

- New urbanist subdivision principles

- Transit corridor planning and enhancements

- Downtown design guidelines

- Neighborhood design guidelines

- Redevelopment master plan areas

In addition, this position will assist the Growth Officer in creating outreach materials and implementing tools that increase the awareness of the role of urban design and result in creating a more livable city. Qualified candidates will have a bachelor's degree in Urban/Environmental Design, Architecture or Landscape Architecture, or a related field, plus five years of related work experience, two of which were in a lead or supervisory capacity. Proficiency with CAD drawing systems, 3-D projection and rendering software, Geographic Information Systems (GIS), Photoshop, PageMaker, Freehand/Illustrator strongly preferred.

Experience required: Five years of relevant experience, two in lead or supervisory role.

Education requirements: Bachelor's degree in Urban/Environmental Design, Architecture or Landscape Architecture, or a related field.

Site Planner, New Jersey

Leading architectural and engineering firm has immediate openings for site planners. Individuals need to perform various tasks including zoning research, site analysis and design, base map preparations, and presentation drawings for retail/commercial sites. Position requires a good knowledge of AutoCAD 14, color rendering abilities, good graphic skills, organizational and communication skills. Candidates should be self-starting team player with multitasking abilities to work in a fast-paced environment. We offer a competitive salary, benefits, and bonus package with an opportunity for career growth in a stable environment.

Experience required: one to four years.

Education requirements: A degree from an accredited college or university in Planning, Landscape Architecture, Architecture, or Civil Engineering.

FIRSTHAND ACCOUNT

Matthew I. Zehnder, Landscape Architect/Regional Planner

Matthew Zehnder works for META Associates, Inc., in Louisville, Kentucky, a health-care-oriented strategic planning and program management firm. He is senior vice president of landscape architecture and community planning. The firm deals primarily with all developmental aspects of health-care-related projects, from the master planning of health-care assisted-living communities to forty-bed private care facilities.

He earned his B.S.L.A. (Bachelor of Science in Landscape Architecture) from the University of Kentucky in Lexington, Kentucky, in 1988. In 1993 he earned a master's degree in landscape architecture and regional planning from the University of Pennsylvania in Philadelphia.

Getting Started

"I was first attracted to the profession with the thought that I would have opportunities to work out-of-doors on occasion. I enjoyed working with plants and was interested in learning how to implement a design using plants as a palette.

"I researched several firms in the community where I wanted to live. I learned as much about each firm as possible, including the firms' partners, so that when I would go on my interviews I could speak intelligently about each firm's accomplishments.

"Eventually, I was approached by a mid-level executive from META Associates, the firm that currently employs me. The person who approached me asked me if I would be interested in leading their planning department. I was, indeed, interested and began what was to be a six-month interview process.

"I was interviewed by all three partners separately for approximately two hours per interview. I was essentially allowed to espouse my views and ideas concerning design and how I market myself and the firms I have represented in the past.

"After my last individual interview, I was then asked to attend a luncheon with all the partners in attendance. They asked me about my specific goals for my career and what I would like to accomplish in my design life.

"After that I was asked to draft a business plan and forecast a figure of billable hours for myself. Following my producing this document, there was a final interview during which I presented my requirements for employment. Our negotiations following this meeting culminated in a written offer that I accepted."

What the Work Is Like

"My job is the most wonderful job I could have imagined! I set my own hours—within reason. I answer to one partner and am responsible for myself. My job is a little unusual in that I have pursued the marketing and contractual administration path that it seems few LA's pursue.

"My typical day begins at 9:00 in the morning. I listen to my voice mail and promptly answer them all. I then write around ten notes to different business associates and friends so that my network line remains open and up to date. The three most important words: network, network, network!

"If I am not working on a proposal, then I am completing a schematic design or I am making appointments to visit with people I think my firm could provide a service to.

"I do not spend a lot of time drawing. When I first began my LA career I ran blueprints and mostly did the grunt work, but eventually, with hard work and experience, I progressed to executive management.

"My job keeps me moving, both locally and nationally, and my workweek averages about sixty-five hours a week. I do not bring work home. My position is very corporate, yet I depend on many individuals to assist me in completing my job; that is, you must be willing to believe that there are others who can do just as good a job as you, or better. I travel to the job sites frequently. My firm competes nationally, so I log approximately 120,000 miles a year in the sky. The work atmosphere is very user-friendly and open. Everyone freely comments about your design ideas and makes suggestions, when warranted, on ways to improve a design.

"I enjoy the freedom my employer permits me. I enjoy the trust my employer puts in me, and I enjoy the varied design professionals I interact with. The least enjoyable part of my job is the paperwork and the complicated time-sheet processes."

**Advice from
Matthew Zehnder**

"Know what you want to do and where you want to be throughout the course of your life. It is essential to write down a set of goals to reach in five years and continue to review your goals and adjust them as necessary. In this field, you must decide between the academic world and the professional world of this profession—they are two very different worlds, so you should thoroughly research each area. Pick the firm you want to work for and pursue it like it's the last place in the world to work. And the most important item—believe in what you want to do and do it!"

CONSTRUCTION

Some architects move into careers in construction, working as contractors, construction managers, cost estimators, or providers of design/build services. These careers require experience in materials and products and their costs; labor and labor relations; construction planning and logistics; and construction equipment, scheduling, and operations.

DUTIES OF CONSTRUCTION MANAGERS

Construction managers assume a wide variety of responsibilities and positions within construction firms and are known by a range of job titles that are often used interchangeably. For example, a construction manager may also be known as a construction superintendent, general superintendent, project manager, general construction manager, or executive construction manager.

Construction managers may be owners or salaried employees of a construction management or contracting firm, or individuals working under contract or as salaried employees for the owner, developer, contractor, or management firm overseeing the construction project. Here we'll use the term *construction manager* to encompass all supervisory-level salaried and self-employed construction managers who oversee construction supervisors and workers.

In the construction industry, managers and other professionals active in the industry—general managers, project engineers, cost estimators, and others—are increasingly referred to as *constructors*. The term *constructor* refers to a broad group of professionals in construction who, through education and experience, are capable of managing, coordinating, and supervising the construction process from conceptual development through final construction on a timely and economical basis. Given designs for buildings, roads, bridges, or other projects, constructors oversee the organization, scheduling, and implementation of the projects to execute those designs. They are responsible for coordinating and managing people, materials, and equipment; budgets, schedules, and contracts; and the safety of employees and the general public.

The term *construction manager* is also used more narrowly within the construction industry to denote a firm, or an individual employed by the firm, involved in management oversight of a construction project. Under this narrower definition, construction managers generally act as agents or representatives of the owner or developer throughout the life of the project. Although they generally play no direct role in the actual construction of the building or other facility, they typically schedule and coordinate all design and construction processes. They develop and implement a management plan to complete the project according to the owner's goals that allows the design and construction processes to be carried out efficiently and effectively within budgetary and schedule constraints.

Generally, a contractor is the firm under contract to provide specialized construction services. On small projects such as remodeling a home, the construction contractor is usually a self-employed construction manager or skilled trade worker who directs and oversees employees. On larger projects, construction managers working for a general contractor have overall responsibility for completing the construction in accordance with the engineer's or architect's drawings and specifications and prevailing building codes. They arrange for subcontractors to perform specialized craft work or other specified construction work.

Large construction projects, such as an office building or industrial complex, for example, are too complicated for one person to supervise. These projects are divided into many segments: site preparation, including land clearing and earth moving; sewage systems; landscaping and road construction; building construction, including excavation and laying foundations, erection of structural framework, floors, walls, and roofs; and building systems, including fire protection, electrical, plumbing, air-conditioning, and heating. Construction managers may work as part of a team or may be in charge of one or more of these activities. They may have several subordinates, such as assistant project managers, superintendents, field engineers, or crew supervisors, reporting to them.

Construction managers plan, budget, and direct the construction project. They evaluate various construction methods and determine the most cost-effective plan and schedule. They determine the appropriate construction methods and schedule all required construction site activities into logical, specific steps, budgeting the time required to meet established deadlines. This may require sophisticated estimating and scheduling techniques, using computers with specialized software. Construction managers determine the labor requirements and, in some cases, supervise or monitor the hiring and dismissal of workers.

Managers direct and monitor the progress of field or site construction activities, at times through other construction supervisors. This includes the delivery and use of materials, tools, and equipment; the quality of construction, worker productivity, and safety. They are responsible for obtaining all necessary permits and licenses and, depending upon the contractual arrangements, direct or monitor compliance with building and safety codes and other regulations.

They regularly review engineering and architectural drawings and specifications to monitor progress and ensure compliance with plans and specifications. They track and control construction costs to avoid cost overruns. Based upon direct observation and reports by subordinate supervisors, managers may prepare daily reports of progress and requirements for labor, material, and machinery and equipment at the construction site.

Construction managers work out of a main office from which the overall construction project is monitored or out of a field office at the construction site. While construction managers meet regularly with owners, subcontractors, architects, and other design professionals to monitor and coordinate all phases of the construction project, management decisions regarding daily construction activities are usually made at the job site. Managers usually travel when the construction site is in another state or when they are responsible for activities at two or more sites. Management of construction projects overseas usually entails temporary residence in another country.

Construction managers must be "on call" to deal with delays, bad weather, or emergencies at the site. Most work more than a standard forty-hour week since construction may proceed around-the-clock. This type of work schedule can go on for days, even weeks, to meet special project deadlines, especially if there have been unforeseen delays.

Although the work generally is not considered dangerous, construction managers must be careful while touring construction sites, especially when large machinery, heavy equipment, and vehicles are being operated. Managers must be able to establish priorities and assign duties. They need to observe job conditions and to be alert to changes and potential problems, particularly involving safety on the job site and adherence to regulations.

TRAINING FOR CONSTRUCTION MANAGERS

Students may pursue baccalaureate or advanced degrees in building sciences, construction, and construction management. Some of these programs are offered in architecture schools, others in engineering or separate construction schools. The American Council for Construction Education accredits academic programs in construction.

People interested in becoming construction managers need a solid background in building science, business, and management, as well as related work experience within the construction industry. They need to understand contracts, plans, and specifications, and to be knowledgeable about construction methods, materials, and regulations. Familiarity with computers and software programs for job costing, scheduling, and estimating is increasingly important.

Traditionally, people advance to construction management positions after having substantial experience as construction craft workers—carpenters, masons, plumbers, or electricians, for example—or after having worked as construction supervisors or as owners of independent specialty contracting firms overseeing workers in one or more construction trades. However, more and more employers—particularly, large construction firms—hire individuals who combine industry work experience with a bachelor's degree in construction or building science or construction management. Practical industry experience is very important, whether through internships, cooperative education programs, or tenure in the industry.

More than 100 colleges and universities offered four-year degree programs in construction management or construction science. These programs include courses in project control and development, site planning, design, construction methods, construction materials, value analysis, cost estimating, scheduling, contract administration, accounting, business and financial management, building codes and standards, inspection procedures, engineering and architectural sciences, mathematics, statistics, and information technology.

Graduates from four-year degree programs are usually hired as assistants to project managers, field engineers, schedulers, or cost estimators. An increasing number of graduates in related fields—engineering or architecture, for example—also enter construction management, often after having had substantial experience on construction projects or after completing graduate studies in construction management or building science.

Around thirty colleges and universities offer a master's degree program in construction management or construction science, and at least two offer a Ph.D. in the field. Master's degree recipients, especially those with work experience in construction, typically become construction managers in very large construction or construction management companies. Often, individuals who hold a bachelor's degree in an unrelated field seek a master's degree to work in the construction industry. Doctoral degree recipients usually become college professors or conduct research.

CERTIFICATION FOR CONSTRUCTION MANAGERS

Both the American Institute of Constructors (AIC) and the Construction Management Association of America (CMAA) have established voluntary certification programs for construction professionals. Requirements combine written examinations with verification of professional experience. AIC awards the designations Associate Constructor (AC) and Certified Professional Constructor (CPC) to candidates who meet the requirements and pass appropriate construction examinations. CMAA awards the designation Certified Construction Manager (CCM) to practitioners who meet the requirements in a construction management firm, complete a professional construction management "capstone" course, and pass a technical examination. Although certification is not required to work in the construction industry, voluntary certification can be valuable because it provides evidence of competence and experience.

SALARIES FOR CONSTRUCTION MANAGERS AND CONTRACTORS

Earnings of salaried construction managers and self-employed independent construction contractors vary depending upon the size and nature of the construction project, its geographic location, and economic conditions. In addition to typical benefits, many salaried construction managers receive benefits such as bonuses and use of company motor vehicles.

Median annual earnings of construction managers are $47,610. The middle 50 percent earn between $36,360 and $70,910. The lowest 10 percent earn less than $28,970, and the highest 10 percent earn more than $89,480. Median annual earnings in the industries employing the largest numbers of managers are:

Plumbing, heating, and air-conditioning $47,000

Nonresidential building construction   47,700

Heavy construction, except highway   45,700

Miscellaneous special trade contractors 44,200

Residential building construction   40,600

According to a 1999 salary survey by the National Association of Colleges and Employers, candidates with a bachelor's degree in construction management received offers averaging $34,300 a year. Bachelor's degree candidates with degrees in construction science received offers averaging $36,600.

JOB OUTLOOK FOR CONSTRUCTION MANAGERS

Construction managers hold about 270,000 jobs nationwide. Around 45,000 of that figure are self-employed. About 85 percent of salaried construction managers are employed in the construction industry, about 36 percent by specialty trade contractors—for example, plumbing, heating and air-conditioning, and electrical contractors—and about 38 percent by general building contractors. Engineering, architectural, and construction management services firms, as well as local governments, educational institutions, and real estate developers employed others.

According to the U.S. Bureau of Labor Statistics, employment of construction managers is expected to increase about as fast as the average for all occupations through 2008, as the level and complexity of construction activity continues to grow. Prospects in construction management, engineering and architectural services, and construction contracting firms should be best for people who have a bachelor's or higher degree in construction science, construction management, or construction engineering as well as practical experience working in construction.

Employers prefer applicants with previous construction work experience who can combine a strong background in building technology with proven supervisory or managerial skills. In addition to job growth, many openings should result annually from the need to replace workers who transfer to other occupations or leave the labor force.

The increasing complexity of construction projects should increase demand for management level personnel within the construction industry, as sophisticated technology and the proliferation of laws setting standards for buildings and construction materials, worker safety, energy efficiency, and environmental protection have further complicated the construction process. Advances in building materials and construction methods and the growing number of multi-purpose buildings, electronically operated "smart" buildings, and energy-efficient structures will further add to the demand for more construction managers. However, employment of construction managers can be sensitive to the short-term nature of many construction projects and cyclical fluctuations in construction activity.

DUTIES OF COST ESTIMATORS

Accurately forecasting the cost of future projects is vital to the survival of any business. Cost estimators develop cost information for owners or managers to use in determining resource and material quantities, making bids for contracts, determining if a new product will be profitable, or determining which products are making a profit for a firm.

Regardless of the industry in which they work, estimators compile and analyze data on all the factors that can influence costs, such as materials, labor, location, and special machinery requirements, including computer hardware and software. Job duties vary widely depending on the type and size of the project. Costs engineers usually have an engineering background and apply scientific principles and methods to undertake feasibility studies, value engineering, and life-cycle costing. Because computers play an integral role in cost estimating, you should possess strong computer skills. Estimating may involve complex mathematical calculations and require advanced mathematical techniques.

Construction cost estimators may also be employed by the project's architect or owner to estimate costs or track actual costs relative to bid specifications as the project develops. In large construction companies employing more than one estimator, it is common practice for estimators to specialize. For instance, one may estimate only electrical work and another may concentrate on excavation, concrete, and forms.

TRAINING FOR COST ESTIMATORS

Entry requirements for cost estimators vary by industry. In the construction industry employers increasingly prefer individuals with a degree in building construction, construction management, construction science, engineering, or architecture. However, most construction estimators also have considerable construction experience, gained through tenure in the industry, internships, or cooperative education programs. Applicants with a thorough knowledge of construction materials, costs, and procedures in areas ranging from heavy construction to electrical work, plumbing systems, or masonry work have a competitive edge.

Cost estimators should have an aptitude for mathematics, be able to quickly analyze, compare, and interpret detailed and sometimes poorly defined information, and be able to make sound and accurate judgments based on this knowledge. Assertiveness and self-confidence in presenting and supporting their conclusions are important, as are strong communication and interpersonal skills, because estimators may work as part of a project team alongside managers, owners, engineers, and design professionals. Cost estimators also need knowledge of computers, including word-processing and spreadsheet packages. In some instances, familiarity with special estimation software or programming skills may also be required.

Regardless of their background, estimators receive much training on the job; almost every company has its own way of handling estimates. Working with an experienced estimator, they become familiar with each step in the process. Those with no experience reading construction specifications or blueprints first learn that aspect of the work. They then may accompany an experienced estimator to the construction site or shop floor where they observe the work being done, take measurements, or perform other routine tasks. As they become more knowledgeable, estimators learn how to tabulate quantities and dimensions from drawings and how to select the appropriate material prices.

For most estimators, advancement takes the form of higher pay and prestige. Some move into management positions, such as project manager for a construction firm or manager of the industrial engineering department for a manufacturer. Others may go into business for themselves as consultants, providing estimating services for a fee to government or construction and manufacturing firms.

Many colleges and universities include cost estimating as part of bachelor's and associate degree curriculums in civil engineering, industrial engineering, and construction management or construction engineering technology. In addition, cost estimating is a significant part of many master's degree programs in construction science or construction management. Organizations representing cost estimators, such as the American Association of Cost Engineers (AACE) International and the Society of Cost Estimating and Analysis, also sponsor educational and professional development programs. These programs help students, estimators-in-training, and experienced estimators stay abreast of changes affecting the profession. Specialized courses and programs in cost estimating techniques and procedures are also offered by many technical schools, community colleges, and universities.

CERTIFICATION FOR COST ESTIMATORS

Voluntary certification can be valuable to cost estimators, because it provides professional recognition of the estimator's competence and experience. In some instances, individual employers may even require professional certification for employment. Both AACE International and the Society of Cost Estimating and Analysis administer certification programs. To become certified, estimators usually must have between three and seven years of estimating experience and must pass both a written and an oral examination. In addition, certification requirements may include publication of at least one article or paper in the field.

SALARIES FOR COST ESTIMATORS

Salaries of cost estimators vary widely by experience, education, size of firm, and industry. Median annual earnings of cost estimators are $40,590. The middle 50 percent earn between $31,270 and $53,490. The lowest 10 percent earn less than $24,330, and the highest 10 percent earn more than $79,400. Median annual earnings in the industries employing the largest numbers of managers are:

Nonresidential building construction	$43,400
Electrical work	43,400
Plumbing, heating, and air-conditioning	40,700
Miscellaneous special trade contractors	39,200
Residential building construction	35,300

You should keep in mind that college graduates with degrees in fields such as engineering or construction management that provide a strong background in cost estimating could start at a higher level than those cited above.

According to a 1999 salary survey by the National Association of Colleges and Employers, bachelor's degree candidates with degrees in construction science received offers averaging about $36,600 a year. Bachelor's degree candidates with degrees in construction management received offers averaging $34,300 a year.

JOB OUTLOOK FOR COST ESTIMATORS

Cost estimators hold about 152,000 jobs nationwide; about 58 percent of those are in the construction industry. Another 26 percent of salaried cost estimators are employed in manufacturing industries. The remainder work for engineering and architectural services firms, business services firms, and throughout a wide range of other industries.

Overall employment of cost estimators is expected to grow about as fast as the average for all occupations through the year 2008. No new projects in construction, manufacturing, or other industries are undertaken without careful analysis and estimation of the costs involved. In addition to openings created by growth, some job openings will also arise from the need to replace workers who transfer to other occupations or leave the labor force.

Growth of the construction industry, where more than half of all cost estimators are employed, will be the driving force behind the demand for these workers. The fastest growing sectors of the construction industry are expected to be special trade contractors and those associated with heavy construction and spending on the nation's infrastructure. In addition, construction and repair of highways, streets, and bridges and construction of more subway systems, airports, water and sewage systems, electric power plants, and transmission lines will stimulate demand for many more cost estimators. Job prospects in construction should be best for cost estimators with a degree in construction management or construction science, engineering, or architecture who have practical experience in various phases of construction or in a specialty craft area.

Employment of cost estimators in manufacturing should remain relatively stable as firms continue to use their services to identify and control their operating costs. Experienced estimators with degrees in engineering, science, mathematics, business administration, or economics and who have computer expertise should have the best job prospects in manufacturing.

SAMPLE JOB LISTING

This listing is provided as a sample only, and as such, the hiring firm is not mentioned. You may find similar listings by doing an Internet search using keywords such as "jobs" and "construction" or "contracting."

Estimators and Senior Contracting, California

Estimators who are experienced in mid- and high-rise buildings are needed to develop conceptual designs, forming costs, prepare firm fixed-price bids, and perform material scheduling and planning for precast wall systems. You will meet with architects, owners, and general contractors, so your experience with precast concrete and a civil engineering degree with ten to twenty years' experience is most helpful.

FIRSTHAND ACCOUNTS

Lee Sullivan Hill, Cost Estimator

Lee Sullivan Hill works for Turner Construction Company, an international construction management and general contracting firm headquartered in New York City. Lee worked in the Washington, D.C., office for seven years, in Connecticut for two years, and is now in Chicago, Illinois.

Getting Started

"As a child, I had never in my life met an engineer. I did not even know what one was. I did, however, love architecture. My grandmother's father had been an 'architect,' and time spent on walks with her taught me to look for mansard roofs and Doric columns by age five.

"Fast-forward to my freshman year in college. My roommate was an engineering student, and I became intrigued by her homework assignments—they looked so interesting. I had always been good at math and interested in architecture, so I decided, three weeks into my sophomore year, to switch to an engineering concentration. The AB engineering program at Lafayette allowed me to take civil engineering courses such as Structures and Design of Small Dams as well as art classes, history, English, and French.

"I had planned to go to graduate school for architecture, but my boyfriend, my husband-to-be, graduated two years before I did and went to work with Turner Construction. I loved hearing about his job, which was building a dormitory at Gallaudet College in D.C. By the time May rolled around, I had found my niche. I received offers from other construction firms, but chose Turner.

"I started with Turner right out of college, and my first assignments were on construction job sites where I was assigned to the Cost Estimating Department. I left to become a stay-at-home mom for several years. When I returned to work, I resumed my estimating duties on a part-time, hourly basis. I have done just one estimate for Turner since moving to Chicago in April of 1996 because my 'other' career, writing children's books, has accelerated.

"The training at Turner took me through work on job sites, but I naturally gravitated toward estimating. Even on my first job where I laid out concrete for a water treatment plant, I did take-off and labor studies. My work was neat, organized, and thorough.

"The training within estimating was mostly one-on-one with my boss. The department had four people in it and included the chief, so there was plenty of time for this method. My natural talents for organizing information made the learning simple. In 1982, when I started, computers were not yet a factor, however, it became my job in 1985 and 1986 to computerize the department and provide training to the other estimators. My boss started me out counting door-frames and windows, and pretty soon I was taking on small projects of my own.

"Turner Construction has a formalized training program of seminars that contributed greatly to my knowledge, while reading trade journals and talking with subcontractors about their work added finishing touches."

What the Work Is Like   "All estimators spend time reviewing drawings and specifications for upcoming construction projects. They study the plans, read the specs, take notes on unusual (maybe expensive) details, make lists of questions and qualifications, and envision the finished building. They might ask themselves, what problems will arise during construction? What has the architect left out of the design that will be needed to finish the work? Can we change some details that will save the owner money and still provide a quality building? Are there some details we know cause major problems (such as rainwater seeping through bad flashing details) that we should pay attention to?

"Secondly, all estimators count. They use digitizers that count with computer programs or they count with their fingers, but all estimators must figure out, for each project, how many square feet, cubic yards, or linear feet are required. This computation must be done in an organized fashion, and it must be checked and rechecked.

"Thirdly, all estimators assign prices to the work. For every item they counted, they assign a price. This is more complicated than you may imagine. It's not just running to a fat book and pulling out a price. Every job has specifics that may make prices higher or lower. For example, one must consider if the work will take place during the winter and require extra money for heat, or if new labor contracts coming up might change the costs of the whole project, or take into consideration insurance requirements. All the details must be compared. Subcontractors called on the phone can offer advice, and discussions with the owner and architect may clarify unknowns.

"This brings us to the most important task of all: communication. All the organized notes and careful pricing and checking of work and rechecking of work are nothing without communication. Final reports, or lump sum bids, or meetings with owners before construction starts, are all critical components of an estimator's job.

"On large projects, the estimate is broken into pieces and assigned to several estimators. The lead estimator must communicate with everyone and pull the information together without dropping a piece that might cost big money later. The ability to communicate is hard to train into people. Companies look for this quality in all of those hired.

"In summary, estimating is a fun, stimulating, exciting process that involves seemingly opposite activities—individual activities such as thinking and counting, and group activities that require communication with others, such as contacting subcontractors, owners, architects, and people within your own company. This job is never boring."

The Upsides and Downsides

"I loved seeing plans for new buildings, imagining their beauty, imagining the smell of the concrete foundations freshly poured, the wood floors freshly varnished.

"The only real downside was that sometimes you'd bust your gut for a month on a project, and put in a price/bid and find out that another contractor was given the job for a million dollars less than you projected."

Salaries

"I am paid hourly, which is not the norm for this field, and I receive $25 an hour. Turner happens to be flexible and has found that this is a way to keep good women engineers who want to balance family and career. They also give an end-of-year bonus proportional to your salary. A full-time estimator would be paid on a salary and make anywhere from $40,000 to $100,000—it really depends upon years of experience and level."

Advice from Lee Sullivan Hill

"Study civil engineering, construction management, or architecture in college. Get as much work experience related to the field as you can during the summers. Even being a laborer on a job site counts as construction experience when you look for your job at graduation. And hone your communication (both written and verbal) skills. They will serve you better than anything you could write in your resume."

Steve Lazarian, Licensed General Contractor

Steve Lazarian is owner and president of CityWorks, Inc., located in Pasadena, California. In 1970 he earned his B.A. in economics and business from Westmont College in Montecito, California, and in 1973 his law degree from Cal Western School of Law in San Diego, California. He is also a licensed real estate broker and has been in the field since 1972.

Getting Started

"I grew up in a construction atmosphere. My father started an electrical construction business in 1948. I worked as a kid, sweeping the warehouse, and then later in the office in purchasing, estimating, and accounting. The business became very successful, but I was not interested in the technical aspects of the business so I went to law school. After graduating, passing the Bar, and starting my own practice, I realized that I was most interested in construction law. I developed a clientele with contractors, subcontractors, developers, and real estate brokers.

"After my appointment to the Contractor's State License Board in 1985, I became interested in the business itself. Our family started a general construction business in 1983 that was becoming successful and growing fast. In 1989, I decided to leave my practice and manage the general construction company, called Crown City Construction, which was liquidated in 1995. That same year I established my own construction company called CityWorks.

"My training came from my business degree, law degree, practice of law, serving on the Contractor's Board, and working in my father's business."

What the Work Is Like

"My duties include overseeing the jobs we construct and the management of construction projects, some of which we perform services for before construction actually commences. I usually start my day by outlining my priorities of what I need to accomplish on that day. This includes confirming meetings and responsibilities of other members of the staff. I spend much of my time preparing spreadsheets, writing contracts, communicating with subcontractors, authorizing payments to subs and vendors, visiting job sites, and working with owners, architects, engineers, and related parties.

"Construction is a very high-risk business. You cannot afford to relax at any time. There is no time to even be 'busy-relaxed.' I need every moment of the day to stay on top of the many pitfalls that can cause one to fail in this business. That is one reason that I firmly believe in being extremely organized. That allows me to cover the numerous project-related items that need attention. Each construction job is like operating a separate business because it requires all of the effort and energy of running multiple businesses at the same time. That keeps the pace very fast and exciting and, of course, there is the personal reward at the end of the job of seeing the structure that you have built in its completed form.

"The business of construction is very interesting. When we took over the construction of the Los Angeles Mission in downtown Los Angeles from the contractor who had failed on the job, we realized the need for construction management and preconstruction services. We started to render those services in earnest during the past seven years, and it has proven to be the most interesting aspect of the work for me. We are able to assist the owners during the planning stage, which helps save them money and time. That allows us to be very professional in an industry that is not very professional."

The Upsides and Downsides

"The most rewarding part of the business is helping people meet their needs in planning and building structures for them. The business is very people-oriented. You are constantly in dialogue with people all day, every day, so you must be able to work with people. You need to possess team spirit because you perform your work along with many others.

"The ability to communicate is a necessary skill in this field. Since my background and training is in communication and leading effectively by written and spoken word, I enjoy this part of the business.

"The worst part of this business is the dishonesty within the industry. Many companies do not care how they get a job or what it takes to convince an owner of their abilities. They will lie, cheat, and steal to convince an owner to give them the work. Many of these unscrupulous contractors could make as much money by being honest, but it seems to be endemic of the business."

Salaries

"While salaries vary, most project managers earn from $30,000 to $65,000 per year, depending upon education and experience. Superintendents make $45,000 to $60,000 per year, depending upon experience. My earnings are in the six figures, but keep in mind that I do the legal work for the company, too."

Advice from Steve Lazarian

"My advice to someone who wants to get into the business is to first obtain a degree in construction management, engineering, or a similar field. Even a degree in communications or literature would be helpful because any degree that helps train you to be able to write and communicate will give you an advantage.

"You must possess people skills, and you should be able to react to situations quickly. If you are interested in the field, you obviously need physical skills."

"If management is a goal, a graduate degree in law, business management, or finance would be helpful. There has been very little consolidation of businesses within the construction industry, mainly because the sophistication of management is not there. Once that changes, there will be a greater need for skilled management personnel with graduate degrees. At the entry level, you will need education and experience. The sooner you get that, the easier it will be to get started in the business so, while going to school, you might consider working part-time for a construction company or taking an internship during the summer vacation periods."

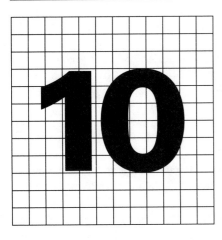

MORE FIRSTHAND ACCOUNTS FROM THE FIELD

In order to get a good idea of what life is like on a daily basis for those working in the exciting and diverse field of architecture, professionals from a range of backgrounds have been interviewed for this book. You'll read about men and women working on large-scale industrial projects and custom homes for individual families. These professionals came to this industry in a variety of unique and interesting ways. They offer words of advice to those considering entering this field that you would be wise to consider.

We wish you the best of luck in establishing a successful and satisfying career in the field of architecture!

Jasper (Joe) Hardesty, Architect

Jasper (Joe) Hardesty is the owner of his own firm, Ecotecture, in Albuquerque, New Mexico. He's involved in commercial and institutional architecture, as well as urban planning. He earned his B.S. in architectural studies from the University of Illinois at Urbana-Champaign and has been working in the field since 1981.

Getting Started

"It was always my intention to enter a field involving science. I was strongly encouraged by my instructors in high school to pursue my aptitude in the fine arts. I ultimately decided upon architecture as a synthesis of the two: providing opportunity for creativity and expression, while also presenting a discipline that solved problems and had practical applications.

"The concept of working with others to generate ideas and environments that people would interact with on a regular basis was particularly stimulating. If we can recognize the social and personal levels in our built environment that influence us, a large number of people over a significant time can derive considerable benefit.

"My first job was not with an architectural firm. At the time I graduated, the fields of architecture and construction in the Midwest and the eastern part of the United States were experiencing a depression. Most firms were laying people off and not hiring or even accepting applications.

"My first related employment was with a consulting engineer who specialized in mechanical/plumbing/electrical engineering. I was offered that position after looking for a job for six months, then responding to an ad from the engineer. My interview involved discussions of my education and expectations of employment, then an exam for production drafting, administered by an associate of the firm.

"My current work is as a self-employed sole proprietor. I chose this path after being approached by several different clients; they had work they wanted me to do, but only if I would do so independently. Because I did not want to be involved with any conflict of interest involving the firm I was working for, I resigned that position and began my own practice. I also decided to do this for personal and professional reasons, including a desire to be my own boss, my intent to spend more time with my family, and to pursue planning and architectural interests of my choosing, rather than those of a firm."

What the Work Is Like

"As sole proprietor of a practice, I am the person responsible for decisions regarding all facets of projects, as well as the business. For the business, this means maintaining contacts for possible work, reviewing and administrating contracts, maintaining books for accounting, paying taxes, filing and preparing registration forms, making travel arrangements, billing/collecting from clients, and paying consultants.

"For each project, I am responsible for maintaining budgets and schedules, conceptual development, master-planning and land-use, programming of facilities, developing designs, creating graphic material, coordination with the client and all consultants, verifying compliance with building and zoning codes, overall administration of the design and document processes, generating and reviewing construction documents, completing specifications, preparing bid documents and conducting the bidding process, administrating construction contracts, site surveys of work under construction, and post-occupancy evaluation of completed work.

"All my projects over the past five years have been focused on 'sustainable design.' This essentially means I work with clients who have an interest in design and construction that has minimal negative impact on the natural and social environment. Most work has involved planning and development of ecotourism facilities—small-scale lodges and hotels that are developed with the intent to preserve natural environments and habitats through tourism revenues. I have also been involved in individual homes and subdivision plans for clients who wish to apply environmentally friendly means to residential development.

"All of my work with private firms involved large commercial and institutional projects, including retail stores and malls, factories, housing subdivisions, campus master plans, educational buildings for universities and public schools, medical facilities, museums, offices, and hotels.

"The job is very difficult, although the satisfaction of the work is considerable, even exhilarating. This field requires extensive hours within a discipline that provides little financial reward, so unless you have good business sense and intend to spend much of your time working, you will not make a large amount of money.

"I get up early in the morning (5:00 to 6:00 A.M.) so I can call prospective clients on the east coast, where it is two hours later than in Albuquerque. I will make as many contact calls to generate new business as possible, then follow up each with a letter and other information that may apply specifically to them. I then check messages and E-mail to see what current crisis some client or consultant may be having.

"About every other day there will be some emergency. If there is no crisis, I then check publications and information resources to maintain my technical library and to look for other potential clients and consultants. There will usually be a meeting or two during the day with clients and/or consultants. I will check on the status of projects under construction, visit a job site, and process a pay request from a contractor. There will often be a need for clarifications and/or changes in documents for work that is out to bid or under construction.

"If I am lucky, I will get to do some work on a newer project in the afternoon, or prepare some renderings and information for a presentation, but not usually. I often must call prospective clients on the West Coast midday to catch them in the morning, then call the East Coast again in the afternoon before they finish for the day, then the West Coast again closer to 5:00 P.M. before they finish.

"The primary use of my time in the day is for communicating and coordinating with others when they are available. By evening I can start doing some of my own work. I will prepare a list of people to contact and work to be done to prepare for the next day. Depending on project schedules, I will work on project design or construction documents. Then I will check the work of consultants, review contracts, prepare paperwork, pay bills, and maintain financial records. I will also review the unpaid statements sent to clients, then send new statements and note to call them the next day.

"One reason I started in architecture was because of the challenge of making an art form that was functional. In this respect, the work is very interesting. I have never been bored by architecture, as I like the aspect of being creative one minute, being an administrator the next, and then a technician the next.

"As a sole proprietor, there is no point in counting hours per week; it would be in the range of eighty to a hundred, with an occasional day off (no weekends). When I worked with other firms, from being an intern to a project manager, the typical workweek was about sixty hours per week, while many were between eighty and one hundred, frequently pulling all-nighters to get work done by deadlines.

"This is a good time to mention that the architectural profession has functioned as an intern-based profession, and it has long maintained the attitude that until interns become professionals, they should pay their dues to earn the status of architect. Once one becomes an architect, then the architect is, of course, a professional, working on a salary basis without overtime pay or compensation. This is obviously not true of all firms, but it is prevalent."

Salaries

"As a project manager working with a firm, with fifteen years of experience, I earned about $40,000 a year, with two weeks' vacation a year, with a health plan and no profit sharing. As a sole proprietor, I do not make as much money and income is inconsistent. Inconsistency is also true of many firms, since architecture is considered a 'feast or famine' business. As a result, I have had many friends move to other parts of the country to follow the work.

"The salary structure for architects in general has been very much like that of public school teachers. Interns and draftspersons starting out often make minimum wage. I made twice as much working in a bakery while looking for my first architecture job as I made when I got my job with an engineer. My wife works as an engineer and makes twice what I did, along with great benefits and four weeks' vacation a year."

Advice from Jasper (Joe) Hardesty

"I would advise anyone considering this career to learn about business—it will help you if you have one, and it will help you to promote yourself within a firm if you choose to do that. Since the profession has become more specialized, you should decide what type of work you want to do, determine if there will be a demand for it, then pursue that specialty. Start out working with a large firm. It will usually establish a better initial wage for you, and will expose you more to the business and practice of architecture. Explore the requirements for registration and licensing as an architect. The requirements have become more demanding. It is more similar to becoming a doctor, and less like becoming a lawyer. Get to know some people experienced in architecture—this does not include professors who are paid by having you as a student. Instead, talk to people who are working in architecture, preferably doing what you might like. Recognize that very few architects actually do design work, although I have been fortunate to do a good deal of this in my practice.

"The qualities you should possess include ambition, passion for hard work, excellent communication skills, excellent mediation skills (consultant and contractor administration is often adversarial), the ability to work and produce under stress, self-confidence (criticism is the norm in the design field), the ability to be creative, and intelligence."

Harvey Schorr, Architect

Harvey Schorr is vice president of Maguire Group Inc., an architectural firm in Foxborough, Massachusetts. He earned his B.Arch. in 1966 and his M.Arch. in advanced studies (urban design) in 1972, both from MIT in Cambridge, Massachusetts. He has been working in the field for thirty-five years.

Getting Started

"I used to draw buildings and airplanes as a kid and even remember doing a report on architecture as a career choice in junior high school, so I guess my interest is of long standing. On the other hand, I was intimidated by the prospect of pursuing it, for fear I was not 'artistic' enough. I studied two years of engineering, and that convinced me I wasn't technical enough either. I naively thought airplanes were 'designed' as a sort of visual or aesthetic undertaking. So, since I was at a technical university, I tried architecture somewhat out of desperation; if that hadn't worked out, I would have had to go to law school.

"After spending two years as an undergraduate in aeronautics and astronautics, I decided I needed a change and, by virtue of drafting skills, got a job in an architect's office. That was in the summer of 1962. I really wasn't of much use, but the man who gave me that job, Howard Dutkin, obviously felt some obligation to the next generation. It was a small office with just one other person. As my first assignment, he paid me to sit down and trace drawings for a house that had already been completed and I helped out bordering sheets, running prints, and the like. By the next summer, perhaps as a result of his generosity, he was out of business, but with a year of architectural school to supplement my meager office experience, I was able to get an intern-level job elsewhere.

"To land my current job, I first had to be laid off from my previous job. I wasn't a bad employee; the office just ran out of work. This cycle of boom and bust, feast or famine, is little understood or appreciated by many people considering architectural careers.

"It seems like a lifetime that I've been in architecture. Included in the thirty-five years I've been in this field are two years of graduate school, one-and-a-half years in Italy researching small towns as a Fulbright grantee, about eight years of teaching on a part-time basis, two years as a research assistant at the Joint Center for Urban Studies, investigating measures of housing quality, and interludes building kilns and helping to start a nonprofit center for pottery."

What the Work Is Like

"We are Renaissance people and we like to think we can do anything. Of course, there are some specialized things we are not well equipped to do—hospitals, clean rooms, high-end retail, for example—and others we don't want to do, such as single-family houses. Everything in between is fair game. Actually, our work is oriented toward commercial, institutional, industrial, and transportation-related projects, with lots of renovation to boot.

"I work on a wide variety of projects, but as a manager I am more involved in organizing them than in doing them. That means proposals, contracts, meetings, phone calls, letters, reports, coordination, critiquing, billing, and chasing accounts receivable.

"The work can be interesting and even challenging. It is great when things go smoothly, but that doesn't happen spontaneously; it takes hard work and luck—and sometimes even those are not enough.

"People do not realize how much of architecture is not about drawing pretty pictures. It is more like being a banker than being an artist. An artist must answer only to himself in seeking to realize his or her vision. Architecture, more often than not, is about the 'bottom line,' about profit and return on investment. (It's been suggested that bankers actually do more to shape the built environment than architects.)

"Unfortunately, people, for the most part, are not taught how to do the things that have to be done to run an office or a project. They are ill-equipped in terms of training, and by temperament, to be 'jacks-of-all-trades,' yet that, in a word, is exactly what the job requires at a certain level. People who cannot write are severely handicapped in carrying out the myriad nontechnical tasks architects must perform.

"That brings me to another issue, namely to the process of design, which is, after all, what we are supposed to be doing. Architectural design is typically taught in a way that is comparable to waiting for lightning to strike: you sit around hoping an idea will come, then you run with it. Only when you've invested a lot of time do you discover that the idea perhaps wasn't the right one. I am very interested in using rational methods to define problems, generate alternative solutions, evaluate them in objective ways, and make appropriate choices regarding their implementation. Architectural schools have failed, in my opinion, in trying to give students the basic intellectual tools they need to be productive and successful.

"In general, architects—unlike engineers—do not work by the clock, and may not always be compensated for the work they do. I typically work nine to ten hours per day and all too often six—or even seven—days a week."

Upsides and Downsides   "I almost want to say I'm a people person, but this seems to have fallen out of favor. I like the problem-solving part of design. While it is nice to do things that are aesthetically appealing and look nice in the trade magazines, there is great satisfaction just in organizing space to solve functional needs so people can work more effectively or live more comfortably. In real life, this is a 'team effort,' as they say, which means that a lot can be compromised along the way because of lack of time, lack of money, lack of skill, or lack of desire—or just bad taste.

"The building process is fraught with difficulty. People often joke that the best projects are those that remain in the flat file, that is, never get built. These are the only ones where we can be sure of not having any problems in the field during construction. It is a tough, and often frustrating, profession. Sometimes I think that the ideal time to have been an architect was a century or so ago when, to oversimplify, I imagine they were predominantly upper class, independently wealthy individuals who could design little projects for friends and family without having to worry about making money in the process.

"Another downside: when you work on your own, you have much more control over what you are doing and you can do it as well as you can. As your practice grows, you can do more, but only by delegating responsibility to others and thereby losing control over what you loved doing in the first place. You cease being a designer and become a manager instead. This is the classic existential dilemma."

Salaries

"New graduates can earn $20,000 to $30,000 per year, depending in part on their abilities and in part on where they happen to be located. Capable project architects with fifteen years of experience might be in the $50,000 to $65,000 range, subject to the same caveats. Supervisory and managerial salaries can be one and a half times that, or more—or less, as well. And for a few very rare luminaries, I'm sure compensation is higher than I might even guess, but no one should expect to reach such a level. Salaries depend upon location, demand, talent, and past performance. The climb up the salary ladder can be—or seem— very slow. A lot is learned on the job and, no matter how dedicated you are or how hard you work, it still takes time to acquire knowledge and skills that are gained only through experience."

Advice from Harvey Schorr

"We all have to chart our own course and make the most of the opportunities presented to us. I don't think that there is a cookbook approach to a career path, nor can all the will in the world make someone into what he or she is not. One could study Frank Lloyd Wright, or anyone else, for a lifetime and never be able to fully comprehend or replicate how he did what he did. There are, in fact, many paths to truth and lots of potentially satisfying roles one can play as an architect or as a member of the allied professions. I would include in this everything from weekend carpentry to government service to real estate development.

"I think the outlook is positive, subject to the lack of stability alluded to earlier. Pay is also an issue, to some degree: architects are not particularly well paid, at least in comparison to other professions (doctors, dentists, lawyers, accountants). Admittedly, we are not always focused on pay; we find other avenues of fulfillment and job satisfaction besides money."

David DeCicco, Architect

David DiCicco is a self-employed architect in Taos, New Mexico. He's involved in residential, commercial, industrial, and institutional architecture and community and regional planning. He earned his B.Arch. in 1974 and his M.S.R.P.—Master of Community and Regional Planning—in 1988, both from North Dakota State University in Fargo. He has been working in the field since 1974.

Getting Started

"I did not intend to go to college immediately after high school, but the Vietnam war changed my mind. While I was there, the only curriculum that really interested me was architecture. This was also the field I knew the most about since my father and older brother are both architects.

"While in college, I was a janitor for several buildings, one of which was an architect/engineer's office. I convinced the person in charge to give me a job with their surveying department and eventually worked my way into a project designer position in the architecture department. More recently, I held a position as the Taos County Planning Director, but a new election brought a commission that decided to replace those in office with people favored by the new government. I wanted to stay in Taos, and since I knew many people in the community, I decided to open a planning and architecture practice here in the fall of 1999."

What the Work Is Like

"As a sole proprietor and the only employee, I do everything from establishing client contacts to cleaning the office. Designing buildings and planning communities is incredibly rewarding, but designing a building is just the beginning of what we do. We then have to communicate that design to the builders in a way that will ensure that the client gets the building the architect designed . . . and the building the client paid for.

"Some architects think that producing construction contract documents or working drawings is boring. I look for the creative aspects of our work at every level, even drawing a window detail. I think an architect's design is only as good as the construction details the architect produces to complete the design.

"My typical day starts with an organizational period during which I plan the day and set out goals for what I want to accomplish by a certain time. For example, today I have to produce three tenant plans for an industrial building that requires a large-scale floor plan, elevation, and sections of the construction. I have to plot them on a large-format printer, then have them reproduced at a local print shop and mail them to the client in Boston. I have a client meeting on a new project at 1:30 and a Zoning Board hearing for a client at 5:30. I have to check my account books and keep detailed records of how I spend my time so I can bill my clients fairly. By the time I get home tonight, I will have worked between ten to twelve hours. Although the day sounds hectic, it is busy, yet rewarding. I can see results at day's end.

"During my busy times I work between fifty to sixty hours per week. This is not always the case. If it were, I would be doing something different. There are also times when I have little or no work and spend my time marketing. I've had entire months with no work and then had months where I needed to complete two months' work in one. So it varies and is, therefore, never boring."

Upsides and Downsides

"I like that I am my own boss. I set my schedule, determine what work I will take, and try to help the community as much as possible. I enjoy my pro bono planning work with community organizations in Taos County, and I enjoy seeing a project that started as a vague discussion with the client come to fruition. One of the best parts of the profession is getting to meet and learn about how other people live and work. The downside is that if you are the kind of person who can't say no, you will, like me, end up working seven days per week."

Salaries

"I am currently earning around $40,000 to $50,000 gross. Since I was in public service for fifteen years, teaching and government, my salary is low. I hope to make more as my practice grows."

Advice from David DiCicco

"Architects should be patient and have excellent people skills. You should develop and keep evolving a philosophical connection between your everyday life and your profession. Look at the world around you and see how you can help through community service that uses your profession to make life better for everyone. Most important, understand the consequences of whatever you do as a professional and a person.

"The job outlook is great, especially if you are willing to apply your architectural training to other fields such as planning, interior design, or product design."

George Hallowell, Architect

George Hallowell is vice president of Studio Pacifica, Ltd., an architecture and interior design firm in Seattle, Washington. He and his partner started the firm in 1993. His work involves a mixture of commercial and residential architecture, specializing in acoustically sensitive spaces such as recording studios and home theaters. He earned his B.A. in urban geography (urban planning) from the University of Washington in Seattle, and his Master's of Architecture from the University of Houston in Texas. He has been working in the field since 1983.

Getting Started

"As long as I can remember, certainly since childhood, I have been interested in architecture and building. I have a very early memory of carrying my father's old briefcase around the house with 'architect' handwritten and taped on the side. As I grew up, I was always building and designing forts and tree houses.

"When I first went to college in 1971, I was registered in the undergraduate architecture program. But because of my age and the period in this country's history, I was a bit too rebellious to go along with all the requirements that the architecture program in my university put on incoming freshman. We were required to take a two-year series of support classes prior to being able to attend any architecture studio classes (the fun stuff). After complying with the requirements for various engineering and math classes, I realized that if the college thought that these support classes were what was important about architecture, I was not interested in the program. I graduated in Urban Geography, a sort of multidisciplinary urban planning program.

"After a series of jobs, including the design, construction, and operation of a recording studio, I decided I was still very interested in architecture. I went back to graduate school in architecture in the early 1980s, and have not looked back. My first job in architecture was as an intern in a small architectural design firm. I discovered the job through friends in the university, and worked at that firm during the three years of the master's program.

"Most states require a period of internship before a person may take a licensing exam and become eligible for architectural licensing. In Texas that period was three years; at the end of the internship is a four-day-long licensing exam. During the internship years, I was employed by a licensed architect and received specific components and areas of training. I was also a recording engineer for about seven years in a recording studio in New Orleans, Louisiana, in the late 1970s. That training has allowed our firm to specialize in acoustically sensitive space design.

"One of my fellow students in the graduate architecture program and I had often dreamed of opening our own architecture firm someday. After we both graduated, worked as interns for a number of years, and became licensed as architects, we decided to follow through on that dream."

What the Work Is Like

"As an owner of an small architecture firm, my duties are somewhat different from an architect who works for someone else's firm. Also, a small firm changes what is required of the architect. Everything that goes on in our firm must be done by one of the three of us, so we each have to wear several hats. The only exception to this statement is accounting, which is done by our bookkeeper.

"I work on all the projects that come into the office. Because we tend to specialize in acoustic design or accessibility, my work is usually involved in residential or commercial recording studios, home theaters, film rooms, audio or video facilities, accessibility renovations, or new universal design (architectural design for people with differing physical needs). We work on projects that are altered or built new for wheelchair users (and other mobility devices), sight- or hearing-impaired users, and for people who are not able to use stairs or other physical barriers.

"When we design, one of the three of us usually assumes more of a lead role depending on the type of project. If the project is acoustical in nature, I usually make first contact with the client and begin the information-gathering process. The client often comes to our office for the first meeting, and discusses all of his or her wants and needs for the project. If the project is a new recording studio, we discuss how many rooms the client wants, the equipment the client uses, the acoustical parameters he or she wants us to follow, the look and feel of the building, the number and types of people that will use the building, and all of the other issues that will affect the design.

"The next step usually involves a design session with just the three of us. We sit down and begin to sketch the layout of the building. We think about sight lines (seeing from room to room), ergonomics, movement of people through the spaces, sizes for equipment, light, and the feel and sound of the rooms. When we have one or more floor plan ideas for how the building might work, we meet again with the client. We then begin to think about how the building works in three dimensions. Do the rooms have high ceilings, are the ceilings flat or sloped, what will the rooms feel like, and so on. If the project were a house instead of a recording studio, we would now begin to think about how the house looks from the outside. How tall is it, how is it massed, how does it sit on the site.

"We have to research building codes and other legal requirements of the municipality and state. When we have some ideas for the three-dimensional design of the building, we usually meet again with the client. Somewhere in this step, we also begin to put the design in CAD (computer-aided design). Except for the early sketching process, most of our work in done on the computer. Our office only has one small drafting table, and it is almost never used.

"So we can design a project for a client, we need to get the client. All of us in our firm are involved in the process of marketing. Marketing duties include going out to meet prospective clients, sending letters and E-mails, creating advertisements, writing magazine or newspaper articles, applying for awards, creating job sheets (individual handout sheets describing projects we have designed), responding to requests for information, and creating and managing our website.

"Keeping a small architecture firm running also requires filing, typing, copying, sorting, bookkeeping, hiring and firing, and managing a library of construction materials and information. It also requires keeping our computer system running properly. Although some of these tasks could be done by outside people or services, we do them ourselves.

"My day is usually from 9:00 to 6:00 with an hour for lunch. We usually have ten to twenty-five jobs active at any given time. In other offices I have worked in, the hours and pace of the job can be very different. When I worked in New York, for example, I sometimes worked more overtime than regular time— eighty to ninety hours a week."

Upsides and Downsides   "I like the design portion of the job. I most enjoy creating a floor plan or shape of a building and seeing it come to life in a built project. There is nothing quite like walking through a space that came out of your imagination. But I don't enjoy the hassle over time schedules or payment that is a part of the operation of any small business."

Salaries

"Someone just out of school with a first professional degree in architecture could expect to earn between $10.50 and $14.00 per hour in the urban areas of the Pacific Northwest. That pay range depends on skill, experience, the size of the office, and of course the business climate in the region. A licensed architect with three to five years' experience would probably expect over $40,000 a year, currently in this region."

Advice from George Hallowell

"I think a career in architecture comes from a love of the profession. Most architects did not go into the profession to make a huge salary or get an easy job; they just enjoy the creation process. I don't think that most successful architects were born with some innate talent, but they put in the effort and time to hone their skills.

"Architects often come from a wide variety of backgrounds, from astronomy to zoology, before getting their architectural degree. I found drafting classes in high school useful. I have also enjoyed classes and independent study courses in art and history. I also had part-time jobs in the construction industry (as a carpenter) to learn the trade. These jobs helped me understand the components and systems that go into buildings, but I know many architects who did not follow this process and are quite successful.

"I think overall life experience and that spark of joy in the creation of a new space or form is the key to success. Investigate buildings you like, talk to people in the profession, look into good architecture education programs, and read some of the many good books on the profession.

"The job outlook for young architects in this part of the country is very good right now. Most firms are constantly on the hunt for good people. Architecture, as with any business, is part of the larger economic cycle, however. As new construction is reduced, so are the jobs for architects."

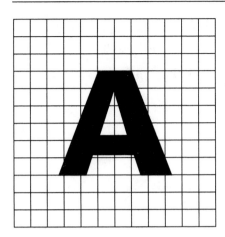

PROFESSIONAL ASSOCIATIONS

Architecture

The American Institute of Architects (AIA) represents the architectural profession and provides resources and tools to its more than 66,000 members.

The AIA has twenty-two professional interest areas such as health-care facilities, the environment, historic resources, interiors, housing, educational facilities, building codes and standards, and international practice.

American Institute of Architects (AIA)
1735 New York Avenue NW
Washington, DC 20006
www.aiaonline.com

Information about education and careers in architecture can be obtained from:

Careers in Architecture Program
American Institute of Architects (AIA)
1735 New York Avenue NW
Washington, DC 20006
www.aiaonline.com

Association of Collegiate Schools of Architecture (ACAS)
1735 New York Avenue NW
Washington, DC 20006
www.acsa-arch.org

The National Architectural Accrediting Board (NAAB), established in 1940, is the sole agency authorized to accredit U.S. professional degrees in architecture.

National Architectural Accrediting Board, Inc. (NAAB)
1735 New York Avenue NW
Washington, DC 20006
www.naab.org

Society of American Registered Architects
1245 South Highland Avenue
Lombard, IL 60148

For more information about registration and internship, write to your state registration board or:

National Council of Architectural Registration Boards (NCARB)
1735 New York Avenue NW
Washington, DC 20006
www.ncarb.org
An Intern Development Program (IDP) information package can be requested by phoning NCARB at (202) 783-6500; or contact your local American Institute of Architects (AIA) chapter or AIA headquarters at (202) 626-7325.

Construction

Information about career opportunities, certification, and educational programs in cost estimating in the construction industry may be obtained from:

AACE International
209 Prairie Avenue, Suite 100
Morgantown, WV 26505

Association of America
P.O. Box 11626
Charlotte, NC 28220-1626

Similar information about cost estimating in government, manufacturing, and other industries is available from:

Society of Cost Estimating and Analysis
101 South Whiting Street, Suite 201
Alexandria, VA 22304

For information about career opportunities in the construction industry, contact:

Associated Builders and Contractors
1300 North Seventeenth Street
Rosslyn, VA 22209
www.abc.org

Associated General Contractors of America
1957 E Street NW
Washington, DC 20006-5199
www.agc.org

For information about constructor certification and professional career opportunities in the construction industry, contact:

American Institute of Constructors
466 Ninety-Fourth Avenue North
St. Petersburg, FL 33702
www.aicnet.org

For information about construction management and construction manager certification, contact:

Construction Management Association of America
7918 Jones Branch Drive, Suite 540
McLean, VA 22102
www.cmaanet.org

Information on accredited construction science and management programs and accreditation requirements is available from:

American Council for Construction Education
1300 Hudson Lane, Suite 3
Monroe, LA 71201-6054
www.acce-hq.org

Engineering

College students interested in obtaining information on professional engineer licensure should contact:

The National Society of Professional Engineers
1420 King Street
Alexandria, VA 22314-2794
www.nspe.org

For those seeking employment with the U.S. government, visit:

www.usajobs.opm.gov

High school students interested in obtaining information on ABET-accredited engineering programs should contact:

The Accreditation Board for Engineering and Technology, Inc.
111 Market Place, Suite 1050
Baltimore, MD 21202-4012
www.abet.org

High school students interested in obtaining general information on a variety of engineering disciplines should contact the Junior Engineering Technical Society, by sending a self-addressed business-size envelope with six first-class stamps affixed to:

JETS-Guidance
1420 King Street, Suite 405
Alexandria, VA 22314-2794
www.jets.org

American Society of Civil Engineers
1801 Alexander Bell Drive
Reston, VA 20191-4400
www.asce.org

American Society of Heating, Refrigerating, and Air-Conditioning Engineers, Inc.
1791 Tullie Circle NE
Atlanta, GA 30329
www.ashrae.org

Electrical and Electronics Engineering

Institute of Electrical and Electronics Engineers—United States of America
1828 L Street NW, Suite 1202
Washington, DC 20036
www.ieeeusa.org

The Minerals, Metals, & Materials Society
184 Thorn Hill Road
Warrendale, PA 15086
www.tms.org

The American Society of Mechanical Engineers
Three Park Avenue
New York, NY 10016
www.asme.org

National Society of Professional Engineers (NSPE)
1420 King Street
Alexandria, VA 22314-2794
www.nspe.org

Historic Preservation

Advisory Council on Historic Preservation
1100 Pennsylvania Avenue NW
Suite 809
Old Post Office Building
Washington, DC 20004
www.achp.gov/mindex.html

The Association for Preservation Technology International (APT)
4513 Lincoln Avenue, Suite 213
Lisle, IL 60532-1290
www.apti.org

The National Register of Historic Places
National Park Service
1849 C Street NW
Washington, DC 20240
www.cr.nps.gov/nr

National Trust for Historic Preservation
1785 Massachusetts Avenue NW
Washington, DC 20036
www.nthp.org

Society of Architectural Historians
1232 Pine Street
Philadelphia, PA 19107
(215) 735-0224

Landscape Architecture

American Forestry Association
P.O. Box 2000
Washington, DC 20013

American Landscape Horticulture Association
2509 East Thousand Oaks Boulevard, Suite 109
Westlake Village, CA 91362

American Society of Landscape Architects
4401 Connecticut Avenue NW, Fifth Floor
Washington, DC 20008-2302
www.asla.org

Associated Landscape Contractors of America
405 North Washington Street #104
Falls Church, VA 22046

Association of Professional Landscape Designers
P.O. Box 134
Kensington, MD 20895

American Society of Landscape Architects
Career Information
636 Eye Street NW
Washington, DC 20001

General information on registration or licensing requirements is available from:

Bureau of Land Management
U.S. Department of the Interior
Room 36191849 C Street NW
Washington, DC 20240

Canadian Society of Landscape Architects
P.O. Box 870, Station B
Ottawa, ON K1P 5P9
Canada
www.csla.ca

Colonial Williamsburg
Employment Office
P.O. Box 1776
Williamsburg, VA 23187

Council of Landscape Architectural Registration Boards
12700 Fair Lakes Circle, Suite 110
Fairfax, VA 22033

Council of Tree and Landscape Appraisers
1250 I Street NW, Suite 504
Washington, DC 20005

Earth Work Student Conservation Association
P.O. Box 550
Charlestown, NH 03603

Golf Course Superintendents Association of America
1421 Research Park Drive
Lawrence, KS 66049-3859

National Landscape Association
1250 Eye Street NW #500
Washington, DC 20005

National Park Service
U.S. Department of the Interior
P.O. Box 37127
Washington, DC 20013-7127

The National Pest Control Association
250 West Jersey Street
Elizabeth, NJ 07207

National Wildlife Federation
1400 Sixteenth Street NW
Washington, DC 20036

Professional Grounds Management Society
10402 Ridgland Road, Suite 4
Hunt Valley, MD 21030

Society of American Foresters
5400 Grosvenor Lane
Bethesda, MD 20814

U.S. Forest Service
U.S. Department of Agriculture
Fourteenth Street and Independence Avenue SW
Washington, DC 20250

World Forestry Center
4033 Southwest Canyon Road
Portland, OR 97221

Monuments

International Council on Monuments and Sites (ICOMOS)
49-51, rue de la Fédération
75015 Paris, France
www.icomos.org/ICOMOS_Main_Page.html
ICOMOS is an international, nongovernmental organization dedicated to the
conservation of the world's historic monuments and sites. The organization was
founded in 1965, as a result of the international adoption of the Charter for the
Conservation and Restoration of Monuments and Sites in Venice the year before.
Today the organization has national committees in over ninety countries.

US/ICOMOS
National Building Museum
401 F Street NW, Room 331
Washington, DC 20001

Terra Cotta

Friends of Terra Cotta, Inc.
c/o Tunick
771 West End Avenue #10E
New York, NY 10025
www.preserve.org/fotc

The Friends of Terra Cotta, Inc., a national nonprofit organization, was founded to promote education and research in the preservation of architectural terra cotta and related ceramic materials. The organization seeks to educate the general public and construction industry professionals about architectural terra cotta's value and history as a building material.

Urban Planning

Information on careers, salaries, and certification in urban and regional planning is available from:

American Planning Association
Education Division
122 South Michigan Avenue, Suite 1600
Chicago, IL 60603
www.planning.org

Additional Associations and Websites
American Association of Botanical Gardens and Arboreta
786 Church Road
Wayne, PA 19087
www.aabga.org

American Concrete Institute
P.O. Box 9094
Farmington Hills, MI 48333
www.aci-int.org

American Consulting Engineers Council
1015 Fifteenth Street NW
Washington, DC 20005
www.acec.org

American Society of Golf Course Architects
221 North LaSalle Street
Chicago, IL 60601
www.services.golfweb.com/library/arch/asgca

American Society of Heating, Refrigerating and Air Conditioning Engineers
    (ASHRAE)
1791 Tullie Circle NE
Atlanta, GA 30329
www.ashrae.org

American Society of Interior Designers (ASID)
608 Massachusetts Avenue NE
Washington, DC 20002-6006
www.asid.org

American Society of Mechanical Engineers
345 East Forty-Seventh Street
New York, NY 10017
www.asme.org

American Subcontractors Association
1004 Duke Street
Alexandria, VA 22314-3588
www.asaonline.com

Architecture Research Institute, Inc.
119 East 35th Street
New York, NY 10016
www.architect.org

Canadian Center for Architecture
1920 Baile Street
Montreal, QC H3H 2S6
Canada
www.cca.qc.ca

Canadian Masonry Research Institute
10524—178 Street, Suite 200
Edmonton, AB T5S 2H1
Canada
www.canmasonry.com

Center for Health Design
3470 Mount Diablo Boulevard
Lafayette, CA 94549
www.healthdesign.org

Center for Resourceful Building Technology
P. O. Box 100
Missoula, MT 59806
www.crbt.org

Construction Industry Computing Association
1 Trust Court, Histon
Cambridge CB4 9PW
England
www.cica.org.uk

Construction Industry Research & Information Association (CIRIA), UK
6 Storey's Gate
London SW1P 3AU
England
www.ciria.org.uk

Construction Innovation Forum
350 South Main Street, Suite 350
Ann Arbor, MI 48104
www.cif.org

Construction Management Association of America
7918 Jones Branch Drive, Suite 540
McLean, VA 22102-3307
www.cmaanet.org

Construction Specifications Institute
99 Canal Center Plaza, Suite 300
Alexandria, VA 22314
www.csinet.org

Council of Educators in Landscape Architecture
Ball State University College of Architecture and Planning
Room #230
Muncie, IN 47306
www.ssc.msu.edu/~la/cela

Council of Landscape Architectural Registration Boards
12700 Fair Lakes Circle, Suite 110
Fairfax, VA 22033
www.clarb.org

Council of Planning Librarians
101 North Wacker Drive, Suite CM-190
Chicago, IL 60606
www.west.asu.edu/mmyers/cpl

Council on Tall Buildings and Urban Habitat
Lehigh University
11 East Packer Avenue
Bethlehem, PA 18015
www.Lehigh.EDU/~inctbuh

Design Management Institute
29 Temple Place, Second Floor
Boston, MA 02111-1350
www.dmi.org

Exhibit Designers and Producers Association
5775 G Peachtree-Dunwoody, Suite 500
Atlanta, GA 30342
www.edpa.com

Foundation for Interior Design Education Research (FIDER)
146 Monroe Center NW, Suite 1318
Grand Rapids, MI 49503-2822
www.fider.org

Frank Lloyd Wright Foundation
Taliesin Wes
P.O. Box 4430
Scottsdale, AZ 85261-4430
www.franklloydwright.org

Frank Lloyd Wright Home & Studio Foundation
951 Chicago Avenue
Oak Park, IL 60302
www.wrightplus.org

Furniture History Society
W. S. Maney & Son Ltd.
P.O. Box YR7
Leeds LS9 7UU
England
www.iserv.net/~plucas/fhsoc.htm

Green Building Council
110 Sutter Street, Suite 410
San Francisco, CA 94104
www.usgbc.org/resource/index.htm

Healthy House Institute
430 North Sewell Road
Bloomington, IN 47408
www.hhinst.com

Historic American Buildings Survey
National Park Service
1849 C Street NW, NC300
Washington, DC 20240
www.cr.nps.gov/habshaer

Illuminating Engineering Society of North America
120 Wall Street, Floor 17
New York, NY 10005
www.iesna.org

Industrial Designers Society of America
1142 Walker Road
Great Falls, VA 22066
www.idsa.org

Industrial Fabrics Association International
1801 County Road B W
Roseville, MN 55113
www.ifai.com

Institute of Electrical and Electronics Engineers (IEEE)
1828 L Street NW, Suite 1202
Washington, DC 20036
www.ieee.org

Institute of Store Planners
25 North Broadway
Tarrytown, NY 10591
www.ispo.org

Institute of Urban and Regional Development
University of California
104 Wheeler Hall #1870
Berkeley, CA 94720-1870
www-iurd.ced.berkeley.edu

International Association of Lighting Designers
Suite 9-104, The Merchandise Mart
200 World Trade Center
Chicago, IL 60654
www.iald.org

International Association of Plumbing and Mechanical Officials
20001 East Walnut Drive South
Walnut, CA 91789-2825
www.iapmo.org

International Building Performance Simulation Association
Member Services Officer: Jeff Haberl, Energy Systems Laboratory
Department of Architecture
Texas A&M University System
College Station, TX 77843-3581
www.mae.okstate.edu/ibpsa

International Code Council
5203 Leesburg Pike, Suite 600
Falls Church, VA 22041
www.intlcode.org

International Council on Monuments and Sites
Secretariat
49-51 rue de la Fédération -75015
Paris, France
www.icomos.org

International Facility Management Association
1 East Greenway Plaza, Suite 1100
Houston, TX 77046-0194
www.ifma.org

International Federation for Housing and Planning
Secretariat
Wassenaarseweg 43
2596 CG The Hague
The Netherlands
www.ifhp.org

International Interior Design Association
Suite 998, The Merchandise Mart
200 World Trade Center
Chicago, IL 60654
www.iida.org

Landscape Design Trust
13a West Street, Reigate
Surrey RH2 9BL
England
www.landscape.co.uk

Landscape Institute (UK)
6–8 Barnard Mews
London SW 11 1QU
England
www.l-i.org.uk

National Association of Environmental Professionals
P.O. Box 2086
Bowie, MD 20718
www.168.143.147.75

National Association of Home Builders Research Center
400 Prince George's Boulevard
Upper Marlboro, MD 20774
www.nahbrc.org

National Association of Industrial and Office Properties
2201 Cooperative Way, Third Floor
Herndon, VA 20171-3034
www.naiop.org

National Association of Home Builders
1201 Fifteenth Street NW
Washington, DC 20005
www.nahb.com

National Association of Housing and Redevelopment Officials
630 Eye Street NW
Washington, DC 20001
www.nahro.org

National Building Museum
401 F Street NW
Washington, DC 20001
www.nbm.org

NCARB Intern-Architect Development Program (IDP)
1801 K Street NW, Suite 1100
Washington, DC 20006
www.ncarb.org/idp

National Organization of Minority Architects
www.students.syr.edu/student_orgs/academic_honorary/omads

National Recreation and Park Association
22377 Belmont Ridge Road
Ashburn, VA 20148
www.nrpa.org

National Renewable Energy Laboratory
1617 Cole Boulevard
Golden, CO 80401-3393
www.nrel.gov

National Research Council of Canada
Institute for Research in Construction
Ottawa, Ontario K1A 0R6
Canada
www.nrc.ca/irc

Organization of Black Designers
300 M Street SW, Suite N110
Washington, DC 20024-4019
www.core77.com/OBD

Partners for Livable Communities
1429 Twenty-First Street NW
Washington, DC 20036
www.livable.com

Partners for Sacred Places
1700 Sansom Street, Tenth Floor
Philadelphia, PA 19103
www.sacredplaces.org

Planners Network
c/o Pratt GCPE
379 DeKalb Avenue
Brooklyn, NY 11205
www.plannersnetwork.org

Planning Advisory Service
122 South Michigan Avenue, Suite 1600
Chicago, IL 60603
www.planning.org/pas/pas.html

Plumbing Heating Cooling Contractors Association
180 South Washington Street
P.O. Box 6808
Falls Church, VA 22040
www.naphcc.org

Rails to Trails Conservancy
1100 Seventeenth Street NW, Tenth Floor
Washington, DC 20036
www.railtrails.org

Regional Plan Association (NY, NJ, CT)
4 Irving Place
New York, NY 10003
www.rpa.org

Royal Institute of British Architects
66 Portland Place
London W1B 1AD
England
www.architecture.com

Society for Environmental Graphic Design
401 F Street NW, Suite 333
Washington, DC 20001
www.segd.org

Society of Architectural Historians of Great Britain
Pixham Mill, Pixham Lane
Dorking, Surrey RH14 1PQ
England
www.sahgb.org.uk/index.html

Solar Energy Industries Association Members Database
1616 H Street NW, Eighth Floor
Washington, DC 20006
www.seia.org/main.htm

Trust for Public Land
116 New Montgomery Street, Fourth Floor
San Francisco, CA 94105
www.tpl.org

UIA International Union of Architects
51, Rue Raynouard - 75016
Paris, France
www.uia-architectes.org

Urban and Regional Information Systems Association
1460 Renaissance Drive, Suite 305
Park Ridge, IL 60068
www.urisa.org

Vernacular Architecture Forum
P.O. Box 1511
Harrisonburg, VA 22801-1511
www.vernaculararchitecture.org/rframe.htm

Wallcoverings Association
401 North Michigan Avenue
Chicago, IL 60611-4267
www.wallcoverings.org

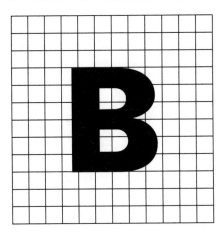

FURTHER READING

Architecture Programs

Guide to Graduate Degree Programs in Architectural History, compiled by Richard Betts. Available through:

Society of Architectural Historians
1232 Pine Street
Philadelphia, PA 19107

The ACSA Publication Guide to Architecture Schools. Completely revised every three to four years, the *Guide* is available in most architecture libraries and bookstores, and can also be ordered directly from ACSA:

Association of Collegiate Schools of Architecture (ACSA)
1735 New York Avenue NW
Washington, DC 20006
www.acsa-arch.org

Architecture Schools: Special Programs

Association of Collegiate Schools of Architecture (ACSA) annually publishes a list of summer programs, *Architecture Schools: Special Programs*:

www.acsa-arch.org

Historic Preservation

Historic Preservation magazine and *Historic Preservation News* published by:

National Trust for Historic Preservation
1785 Massachusetts Avenue NW
Washington, DC 20036
www.nthp.org

Other publications through the National Trust for Historic Preservation include
Challenging Sprawl: Organizational Responses to a National Problem
Getting Started: How to Succeed in Heritage Tourism
*Heritage Resources Law: Protecting the Archeological and Cultural
    Environment*
National Trust Guide to Historic Bed & Breakfasts, Inns, and Small Hotels
Preserving Our Past: Building Our Future
www.nationaltrust.org

Landscape Architecture

Publications from the American Society of Landscape Architects:
Landscape Architecture magazine (LAM)
Landscape Architecture News Digest (LAND)
Landscape Architecture Technical Information Series Online (LATIS Online)
ASLA Reports, Surveys, and Proceedings
www.asla.org.

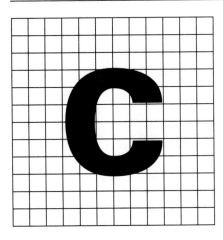

ACCREDITED TRAINING PROGRAMS FOR ARCHITECTURE IN THE UNITED STATES, PUERTO RICO, AND CANADA

United States

Alabama

Auburn University (B.Arch.)
College of Architecture, Design and Construction
202 Dudley Commons
Auburn University, AL 36849-5313
www.auburn.edu/academic/architecture/arch

Tuskegee University (B.Arch.)
Department of Architecture
School of Engineering, Architecture, and Physical Sciences
Tuskegee, AL 36088
www.tusk.edu/colleges/CEAPS/index.html

Arizona

Arizona State University (M.Arch.)
School of Architecture
Tempe, AZ 85287-1605
www.asu.edu/caed/architecture/index.html

Frank Lloyd Wright School of Architecture (M.Arch.)
Taliesin West
Scottsdale, AZ 85261-4430
www.taliesin.edu

University of Arizona (B.Arch.)
College of Architecture, Planning and Landscape
Tucson, AZ 85721
www.architecture.arizona.edu

Arkansas

University of Arkansas (B.Arch.)
School of Architecture
120 Vol Walker Hall
Fayetteville, AR 72701
www.uark.edu/~archhome/school.html

California

California Polytechnic State University, San Luis Obispo (B.Arch.)
College of Architecture and Environmental Design
San Luis Obispo, CA 93407
www.calpoly.edu/~arch

California State Polytechnic University, Pomona (B.Arch, M.Arch)
Department of Architecture
3801 West Temple Avenue
Pomona, CA 91768-4048
www.csupomona.edu/~arc

Southern California Institute of Architecture (B.Arch., M.Arch.)
5454 Beethoven Street
Los Angeles, CA 90066
www.sciarc.edu

University of California, Berkeley (M.Arch.)
Department of Architecture
232 Wurster Hall
Berkeley, CA 94720
www.ced.berkeley.edu:80/arch

University of California, Los Angeles (M.Arch.)
Department of Architecture and Urban Design
1317 Perloff Hall
Los Angeles, CA 90095-1467
www.aud.ucla.edu

University of Southern California (B.Arch.)
School of Architecture
Los Angeles, CA 90089-0291
www.usc.edu/dept/architecture

Woodbury University (B.Arch.)
Department of Architecture
7500 Glenoaks Boulevard
Burbank, CA 91510-7846
www.woodburyu.edu

Colorado

University of Colorado at Denver/Boulder (M.Arch.)
College of Architecture and Planning
Campus Box 126
P.O. Box 173364
Denver, CO 80217-3364
www.cudenver.edu/public/AandP

Connecticut

Yale University (M.Arch.)
School of Architecture
180 York Street
P.O. Box 208242
New Haven, CT 06520
www.architecture.yale.edu

District of Columbia

Catholic University of America (B.Arch., M.Arch.)
School of Architecture and Planning
620 Michigan Avenue NE
Washington, DC 20064
www.cua.edu/www/apu/index.htm

Howard University (B.Arch.)
School of Architecture and Design
2366 Sixth Street NW
Washington, DC 20059
www.imappl.org/CEACS/Departments/Architecture/index.htm

Florida

Florida A&M University (B.Arch., M.Arch.)
School of Architecture
1936 South Martin Luther King Jr. Boulevard
Tallahassee, FL 32307-4200
www.168.223.36.3/acad/college/soa

Florida Atlantic University
777 Glades Road
P.O. Box 3091
Boca Raton, FL 33431
www.fau.edu/dividept/cupa

Florida International University
University Park Campus
11200 SW 8th Street
Miami, FL 33199
www.fiu.edu/index.htm

University of Florida (M.Arch.)
Department of Architecture
P.O. Box 115702
Gainesville, FL 32611-5702
www.arch.ufl.edu

University of Miami (B.Arch., M.Arch.)
School of Architecture
P.O. Box 249178
Coral Gables, FL 33124
www.arc.miami.edu

University of South Florida (M.Arch.)
School of Architecture and Community Design
3702 Spectrum Boulevard, Suite 180
Tampa, FL 33612-9424
www.arch.usf.edu

Georgia

Georgia Institute of Technology (M.Arch.)
College of Architecture
Atlanta, GA 30332-0155
www.arch.gatech.edu

Savannah College of Art and Design (B.Arch.)
Department of Architecture
201 West Charlton Street
Savannah, GA 31401
www.scad.edu

Southern Polytechnic State University (B.Arch.)
School of Architecture
1100 S. Marietta Parkway
Marietta, GA 30060-2896
www.spsuedu/architecture/index.htm

Hawaii

University of Hawaii at Manoa (B.Arch., M.Arch.)
School of Architecture
2410 Campus Road
Honolulu, HI 96822
www.web1.arch.hawaii.edu

Idaho

University of Idaho (B.Arch.)
Department of Architecture
Moscow, ID 83844-2451
www.aa.uidaho.edu/arch

Illinois

Illinois Institute of Technology (B.Arch., M.Arch.)
College of Architecture
S. R. Crown Hall
3360 South State Street
Chicago, IL 60616
www.iit.edu/~arch

University of Illinois at Chicago (B.Arch., M.Arch.)
School of Architecture
845 West Harrison Street, M/C 030
Chicago, IL 60607-7024
www.uic.edu:80/depts/arch/homepage.html

University of Illinois at Urbana-Champaign (M.Arch.)
School of Architecture
Temple Hoyne Buell Hall
611 Taft Drive
Champaign, IL 61820-6921
www.arch.uiuc.edu

Indiana

Ball State University (B.Arch.)
College of Architecture and Planning
Muncie, IN 47306-0305
www.bsu.edu/cap

University of Notre Dame (B.Arch., M.Arch.)
School of Architecture
110 Bond Hall
Notre Dame, IN 46556-5652
www.nd.edu/~arch

Iowa

Iowa State University (B.Arch., M.Arch.)
Department of Architecture
156 College of Design
Ames, IA 50011-3093
www.arch.iastate.edu

Kansas

Kansas State University (B.Arch.)
Department of Architecture
College of Architecture, Planning and Design
Manhattan, KS 66506-2901
www.aalto.arch.ksu.edu

University of Kansas (B.Arch., M.Arch.)
School of Architecture and Urban Design
Lawrence, KS 66045
www.arce.ukans.edu/scharch/scharch.htm

Kentucky

University of Kentucky (B.Arch.)
College of Architecture
Pence Hall
Lexington, KY 40506-0041
www.uky.edu/Architecture

Louisiana

Louisiana State University (B.Arch.)
School of Architecture
College of Design
136 Atkinson Hall
Baton Rouge, LA 70803-5710
www.cadgis.isu.edu/design/index.html

Louisiana Tech University (B.Arch.)
School of Architecture
P.O. Box 3147
Ruston, LA 71272
www.LaTech.edu/tech/arch

Southern University and A&M College (B.Arch.)
School of Architecture
Baton Rouge, LA 70813
www.subr.edu

University of Louisiana at Lafayette (formerly
University of Southwestern Louisiana) (B.Arch.)
School of Architecture
Lafayette, LA 70504-3850
www.arts.louisiana.edu/depts/architecture

Tulane University (B.Arch., M.Arch.)
School of Architecture
Richardson Memorial Hall
New Orleans, LA 70118-5671
www.tulane.edu/~tsahome

Maryland

Morgan State University (M.Arch.)
Institute of Architecture and Planning
Baltimore, MD 21239
www.morgan.edu/academic/schools/archit/archit.htm

University of Maryland (M.Arch.)
School of Architecture
College Park, MD 20742-1411
www.inform.umd.edu/ARCH

Massachusetts

Boston Architectural Center (B.Arch.)
320 Newbury Street
Boston, MA 02115
www.the-bac.edu

Harvard University (M.Arch.)
Department of Architecture
48 Quincy Street
Cambridge, MA 02138
www.gsd.harvard.edu

Massachusetts Institute of Technology (M.Arch.)
Department of Architecture
77 Massachusetts Avenue
Cambridge, MA 02139
www.sap.mit.edu

Wentworth Institute of Technology (B.Arch.)
Department of Architecture
550 Huntington Avenue
Boston, MA 02115-5998
www.wit.edu

Michigan

Andrews University (B.Arch.)
Division of Architecture
Berrien Springs, MI 49104-0450
www.andrews.edu/ARCH

Lawrence Technological University (M.Arch.)
College of Architecture and Design
21000 West Ten Mile Road
Southfield, MI 48075
www.Itu.edu/architecture

University of Detroit, Mercy (B.Arch.)
School of Architecture
P.O. Box 19900
Detroit, MI 48219-0900
www.udmercy.edu

University of Michigan (M.Arch.)
College of Architecture and Urban Planning
Ann Arbor, MI 48109-2069
www.caup.umich.edu

Minnesota

University of Minnesota (M.Arch.)
Department of Architecture
89 Church Street SE
Minneapolis, MN 55455
www.gumby.arch.umn.edu

Mississippi

Mississippi State University (B.Arch.)
School of Architecture
P.O. Drawer AQ
Mississippi State, MS 39762
www.sarc.msstate.edu

Missouri

Drury College (B.Arch.)
Hammons School of Architecture
Springfield, MO 65802
www.drury.edu

Washington University (M.Arch.)
School of Architecture
One Brookings Drive
St. Louis, MO 63130
www.arch.wustl.edu

Montana

Montana State University (B.Arch., M.Arch.)
School of Architecture
Bozeman, MT 59717
www.montana.edu/wwwarch

Nebraska

University of Nebraska (M.Arch.)
College of Architecture
210 Architecture Hall
Lincoln, NE 68588-0106
www.unl.edu/archcoll/index.htm

Nevada

University of Nevada, Las Vegas (M.Arch.)
School of Architecture
4505 Maryland Parkway
Las Vegas, NV 89154-4018
www.nscee.edu/unlv/Colleges

New Jersey

New Jersey Institute of Technology (M.Arch.)
School of Architecture
University Heights
Newark, NJ 07102
www.njit.edu/Directory/Academic/SOA

Princeton University (M.Arch.)
School of Architecture
Princeton, NJ 08544
www.princeton.edu:80/~soa

New Mexico

University of New Mexico (M.Arch.)
School of Architecture and Planning
2414 Central Southeast
Albuquerque, NM 87131
www.unm.edu/~saap

New York

City College of the City University of New York (B.Arch.)
School of Architecture and Environmental Studies
138th Street at Convent Avenue
Shepard Hall 103
New York, NY 10031
www.ccny.cuny.edu

Columbia University (M.Arch.)
Graduate School of Architecture, Planning and Preservation
New York, NY 10027
www.arch.columbia.edu

Cooper Union (B.Arch.)
The Irwin S. Chanin School of Architecture
Cooper Square
New York, NY 10003-7183
www.cooper.edu/architecture/arch.text.html

Cornell University (B.Arch.)
Department of Architecture
143 East Sibley
Ithaca, NY 14853-6701
www.aap.cornell.edu/index.htm

New York Institute of Technology (B.Arch.)
School of Architecture and Design
Old Westbury, NY 11568
www.nyit.edu

Parsons School of Design (M.Arch.)
Department of Architecture
66 Fifth Avenue
New York, NY 10011
www.parsons.edu

Pratt Institute (B.Arch.)
School of Architecture
200 Willoughby Avenue
Brooklyn, NY 11205
www.pratt.edu/arch/index.html

Rensselaer Polytechnic Institute (B.Arch., M.Arch.)
School of Architecture
110 Eighth Street
Troy, NY 12180-3590
www.rpi.edu/dept/arch

State University of New York at Buffalo (M.Arch.)
School of Architecture and Planning
112 Hayes Hall
3435 Main Street
Buffalo, NY 14214-3087
www.ap.buffalo.edu

Syracuse University (B.Arch., M.Arch.)
School of Architecture
103 Slocum Hall
Syracuse, NY 13244-1250
www.mirror.syr.edu/soa.html

North Carolina

North Carolina State University (B.Arch., M.Arch.)
Department of Architecture
Box 7701
Raleigh, NC 27695-7701
www.ncsu.edu/design

University of North Carolina at Charlotte (B.Arch.)
College of Architecture
Charlotte, NC 28223
www.coa.uncc.edu

North Dakota

North Dakota State University (B.Arch.)
Department of Architecture and Landscape Architecture
SU Station, P.O. Box 5285
Fargo, ND 58105
www.ndsu.nodak.edu/arch

Ohio

Kent State University (B.Arch.)
School of Architecture and Environmental Design
200 Taylor Hall
Kent, OH 44242
www.saed.kent.edu/SAED

Miami University (M.Arch.)
Department of Architecture
101 Alumni Hall
Oxford, OH 45056
www.muohio.edu

Ohio State University (M.Arch.)
Austin E. Knowlton School of Architecture
Columbus, OH 43210
www.arch.ohio-state.edu

University of Cincinnati (B.Arch.)
School of Architecture and Interior Design
Cincinnati, OH 45221-0016
www.daap.uc.edu

Oklahoma

Oklahoma State University (B.Arch.)
School of Architecture
Stillwater, OK 74078-5051
www.master.ceat.okstate.edu

University of Oklahoma (B.Arch., M.Arch.)
Division of Architecture
Norman, OK 73019-0265
www.ou.edu/architecture/darch

Oregon

University of Oregon (B.Arch., M.Arch.)
Department of Architecture
School of Architecture and Allied Arts
1206 University of Oregon
Eugene, OR 97403
www.architecture.uoregon.edu/windex.html
Note: The accredited M.Arch. program is offered on both the Eugene and
    Portland campuses.

Pennsylvania

Carnegie Mellon University (B.Arch.)
Department of Architecture
201 College of Fine Arts
Pittsburgh, PA 15213-3890
www.arc.cmu.edu

Drexel University (B.Arch.)
Department of Architecture
Philadelphia, PA 19104
www.coda.drexel.edu/departments/architecture

Pennsylvania State University (B.Arch.)
Department of Architecture
College of Arts and Architecture
206 Engineering Unit C
University Park, PA 16802-1425
www.arch.psu.edu

Philadelphia University (formerly
Philadelphia College of Textiles and Science) (B.Arch.)
School of Architecture and Design
School House Lane and Henry Avenue
Philadelphia, PA 19144-5497
www.philacol.edu/archdes/ad.htm

Temple University (B.Arch.)
Architecture Program
Twelfth and Norris Streets
Philadelphia, PA 19122-1803
www.temple.edu/architecture

University of Pennsylvania (M.Arch.)
Department of Architecture
207 Meyerson Hall
Philadelphia, PA 19104-6311
www.upenn.edu/gsfa

Puerto Rico

University of Puerto Rico (M.Arch.)
School of Architecture
P.O. Box 21909
San Juan, PR 00931-1909

Rhode Island

Rhode Island School of Design (B.Arch., M.Arch.)
Department of Architecture
2 College Street
Providence, RI 02903
www.risd.edu

Roger Williams University (B.Arch.)
School of Architecture
One Old Ferry Road
Briston, RI 02809
www.rwu.edu

South Carolina

Clemson University (M.Arch.)
College of Architecture, Arts, and Humanities
School of Architecture
Clemson, SC 29634-0503
www.hubcap.clemson.edu/aah

Tennessee

University of Tennessee, Knoxville (B.Arch., M.Arch.)
College of Architecture and Planning
Knoxville, TN 37996-2400
www.arch.utk.edu

Texas

Prairie View A&M University (B.Arch.)
Division of Architecture
P.O. Box 397
Prairie View, TX 77446-0397
www.pvamu.edu

Rice University (B.Arch., M.Arch.)
School of Architecture
6100 Main Street, MS #50
Houston, TX 77005-1892
www.arch.rice.edu

Texas A&M University (M.Arch.)
Department of Architecture
College Station, TX 77843-3137
www.archone.tamu.edu

Texas Tech University (B.Arch; M.Arch)
College of Architecture
P.O. Box 42091
Lubbock, TX 79409-2091
www.ttu.edu/~arch

University of Houston (B.Arch., M.Arch.)
Gerald D. Hines College of Architecture
Houston, TX 77204-4431
www.arch.uh.edu

University of Texas at Arlington (M.Arch.)
School of Architecture
Box 19108
Arlington, TX 76019
www.uta.edu/architecture

University of Texas at Austin (B.Arch., M.Arch.)
School of Architecture
Goldsmith Hall 2.308
Austin, TX 78712
www.ar.utexas.edu

Utah

University of Utah (M.Arch.)
Graduate School of Architecture
375 S 1530 E Room 235
Salt Lake City, UT 84112-0370
www.arch.utah.edu

Vermont

Norwich University (B.Arch.)
Division of Architecture and Art
Northfield, VT 05663
www.norwich.edu

Virginia

Hampton University (B.Arch.)
Department of Architecture
Hampton, VA 23668
www.hamptonu.edu

University of Virginia (M.Arch.)
School of Architecture
Campbell Hall
Charlottesville, VA 22903
www.virginia.edu/~arch

Virginia Polytechnic Institute and State University (B.Arch, M.Arch.)
College of Architecture and Urban Studies
Blacksburg, VA 24061-0205

Washington

University of Washington (M.Arch.)
Department of Architecture
Box 355720
Seattle, WA 98195-5720
www.arch.washington.edu/HTML/ARCH

Washington State University (B.Arch.)
School of Architecture
P.O. Box 642220
Pullman, WA 99164-2220
www.arch.wsu.edu

Wisconsin

University of Wisconsin-Milwaukee (M.Arch.)
Department of Architecture
P.O. Box 413
Milwaukee, WI 53201
www.sarup.uwm.edu

CANADA (CACB-ACCREDITED DEGREES)

Carleton University (B.Arch.)
School of Architecture
1125 Colonel By Drive
Ottawa, ON K1S 6B6

Dalhousie University (M.Arch.)
DalTech, Faculty of Architecture
P.O. Box 1000
Halifax, NS B3J 2X4

McGill University (B.Arch.)
School of Architecture
Macdonald-Harrington Building
815 Sherbrooke Street West
Montreal, QC H3A 2K6

Université Laval (B.Arch.)
École d'Architecture
Faculté d'Architecture et d'Aménagement
1 Côte de la Fabrique
Quebec, QC G1K 7P2

Université de Montréal (B.Arch.)
École d'Architecture
Faculté de L'Aménagement
2940, Chemin de la Côte Sainte-Catherine
Bureau 2076
Montreal, QC H3T 1T2

University of British Columbia (M.Arch.)
School of Architecture
6333 Memorial Road
Vancouver, BC V6T 1Z2

University of Calgary (M.Arch.)
Faculty of Environmental Design
2500 University Drive NW
Calgary, AB T2N 1N4

University of Manitoba (M.Arch.)
Faculty of Architecture
201 Russell Building
Winnepeg, MB R3T 2N2

University of Toronto (B.Arch., M.Arch.)
School of Architecture and Landscape Architecture
230 College Street
Toronto, ON N2L 3G1

University of Waterloo (B.Arch.)
School of Architecture
Faculty of Environmental Sciences
Waterloo, ON N2L 3G1

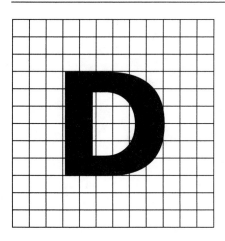

ACCREDITED PROGRAMS IN LANDSCAPE ARCHITECTURE

The Landscape Architectural Accreditation Board (LAAB) is recognized by the Council for Higher Education Accreditation (CHEA) as the accrediting agency for first professional baccalaureate and master's degree programs in landscape architecture in the United States. LAAB is a member of the Association of Specialized and Professional Accreditors.

The Board of Trustees of the American Society of Landscape Architects recognizes the quality of educational programs leading to first professional degrees in landscape architecture at the bachelor's or master's level accredited by the Canadian Society of Landscape Architects Accreditation Council. It regards the criteria for accreditation and many of the individual program guidelines to be comparable to those employed by the Landscape Architectural Accreditation Board of the ASLA. A list of CSLAAC accredited programs follows the LAAB list. LAAB accredits forty-six programs leading to baccalaureate degrees and twenty-nine leading to master's degrees.

United States

Arizona State University (B.S.L.A.)
Landscape Architecture Program
School of Planning and Landscape Architecture
Tempe, AZ 85287-2005

Auburn University (B.L.A.)
School of Architecture
104 Dudley Hall
Auburn, AL 36849-5316
www.auburn.edu/academic/architecture/arch/index.html

Ball State University (B.L.A., M.L.A.)
Department of Landscape Architecture
College of Architecture and Planning
Muncie, IN 47306
www.bsu.edu/cap/landscape/landscape.html

California Polytechnic State University (B.S.L.A.)
Department of Landscape Architecture
College of Architecture and Environmental Design
San Luis Obispo, CA 93407
www.calpoly.edu/~larc

California State Polytechnic University (B.S.L.A., M.L.A.)
Department of Landscape Architecture
College of Environmental Design
3801 West Temple Avenue
Pomona, CA 91768
www.csupomona.edu/~la

City College of New York (B.S.L.A.)
Urban Landscape Architecture Program
School of Architecture and Environmental Studies
138th Street and Convent Avenue
New York, NY 10031

Clemson University (B.L.A.)
Department of Planning and Landscape Architecture
121 Lee Hall, P.O. Box 340511
College of Architecture, Arts and Humanities
Clemson, SC 29634-0511

Colorado State University, B.S.L.A.
Program in Landscape Architecture
Department of Horticulture and Landscape Architecture
College of Agricultural Sciences
Fort Collins, CO 80523
www.hubcap.clemson.edu/aah/pla

Cornell University (B.S.L.A., M.L.A.)
Landscape Architecture Department
440 Kennedy Hall
Ithaca, NY 14853
www.landscape.cornell.edu

Florida International University (M.L.A.)
Graduate Program in Landscape Architecture
School of Architecture
University Park Campus
Miami, FL 33199
www.fiu.edu/~soa

Harvard University (M.L.A.)
Department of Landscape Architecture
Graduate School of Design
409 Gund Hall, 48 Quincy Street
Cambridge, MA 02138
www.gsd.harvard.edu/GSDdep.html

Iowa State University (B.L.A.)
Department of Landscape Architecture
Iowa State University
College of Design, Room 146
Ames, IA 50011
www.public.iastate.edu/~land_arch/homepage.html

Kansas State University (B.L.A., M.L.A.)
Department of Landscape Architecture/Regional and Community Planning
College of Architecture, Planning and Design
302 Seaton Hall
Manhattan, KS 66506-2909
www.aalto.arch.ksu.edu

Louisiana State University (B.L.A., M.L.A.)
School of Landscape Architecture
College of Design Building
Baton Rouge, LA 70803-7020
www.cadgis.lsu.edu/design/LA_HM.html

Michigan State University (B.L.A.)
Landscape Architecture Program
Department of Geography
East Lansing, MI 48824-1221

Mississippi State University (B.L.A.)
Department of Landscape Architecture
College of Agriculture and Life Sciences
P.O. Box 9725
Lloyd Ricks Hall, Room 130
Mississippi State, MS 39762-9725
www.msstate.edu/Dept/LA/public/la_page.html

Morgan State University (M.L.A.)
Graduate Program in Landscape Architecture
Montebello Complex, Room B107
Baltimore, MD 21251
www.jewel.morgan.edu/~jchalk/land

North Carolina A & T State University (B.S.L.A.)
Landscape Architecture Program
231 Carver Hall
Greensboro, NC 27411
www.moore.ncat.edu/NatRes/landarch

North Carolina State University (B.L.A., M.L.A.)
Landscape Architecture Department
School of Design
P.O. Box 7701
Raleigh, NC 27695-7701
www2.ncsu.edu/ncsu/design/sod4/Departments/Landscape/index.html

North Dakota State University (B.L.A.)
Department of Architecture and Landscape Architecture
P.O. Box 5285 S.U. Station
Fargo, ND 58105-5285
www.ndsu.nodak.edu/instruct/dcollito/larchprogram.html

Ohio State University (B.S.L.A., M.L.A.)
Section of Landscape Architecture
Austin E. Knowlton School of Architecture
109 Brown Hall, 190 West Seventeenth Avenue
Columbus, OH 43210-1368
www.arch.ohio-state.edu/larch/wel.htm

Oklahoma State University (B.L.A.)
Landscape Architecture Program, 360 AGH
Stillwater, OK 74078-6027
www.okstate.edu/OSU_Ag/index.html
or www.okstate.edu/OSU_Ag/asnr/hort/index.html

Pennsylvania State University (B.L.A.)
Department of Landscape Architecture
College of Arts and Architecture
210 Engineering Unit D
University Park, PA 16802
www.larch.psu.edu

Purdue University (B.S.L.A.)
Landscape Architecture Program
Department of Horticulture and Landscape Architecture
1165 Horticulture Building
West Lafayette, IN 47907-1165
www.hort.purdue.edu/hort/landarch

Rhode Island School of Design (B.L.A., M.L.A.)
Department of Landscape Architecture
Division of Architecture and Design
2 College Street
Providence, RI 02903

Rutgers—The State University of New Jersey (B.S.)
Department of Landscape Architecture
Blake Hall, Cook College
93 Lipman Drive
New Brunswick, NJ 08901-8524
www.aesop.rutgers.edu/landarch

State University of New York (B.L.A., M.L.A.)
Faculty of Landscape Architecture
College of Environmental Science and Forestry
1 Forestry Drive
Syracuse, NY 13210-2787
www.fla.esf.edu

Temple University (B.S.L.A.)
Department of Landscape Architecture and Horticulture
580 Meetinghouse Road
Ambler, PA 19002-3994

Texas A & M University (B.L.A., M.L.A.)
Department of Landscape Architecture and Urban Planning
College of Architecture
311 Langford Architecture Center
College Station, TX 77843-3137
www.taz.tamu.edu

Texas Tech University (B.L.A.)
Department of Landscape Architecture
College of Agricultural Sciences and Natural Resources
Box 42121
Lubbock, TX 79409-2121

University of Arizona (M.L.A.)
School of Landscape Architecture
Room 104 College of Architecture, Planning and Landscape Architecture
P.O. Box 210075, Room 104
Tucson, AZ 85721-0075
www.architecture.arizona.edu/landscape

University of Arkansas (B.L.A.)
Department of Landscape Architecture
School of Architecture
230 Memorial Hall
Fayetteville, AR 72701

University of California at Berkeley (M.L.A.)
Department of Landscape Architecture
College of Environmental Design
202 Wurster Hall
Berkeley, CA 94720-2000
www.ced.berkeley.edu:80/landscape

University of California at Davis (B.S.L.A.)
Landscape Architecture Program
Department of Environmental Design
College of Agricultural and Environmental Sciences
One Shields Avenue
Davis, CA 95616-8585
www.lda.ucdavis.edu

University of Colorado at Denver (M.L.A.)
Landscape Architecture Program
College of Architecture and Planning
Campus Box 126
P.O. Box 173364
Denver, CO 80217-3364

University of Connecticut (B.S.L.A.)
Landscape Architecture Program
Department of Plant Science
College of Agriculture and Natural Resources
1376 Storrs Road, U-67
Storrs, CT 06269-4067
www.canr.uconn.edu/plsci/la.htm

University of Florida (B.L.A., M.L.A.)
Department of Landscape Architecture
College of Architecture
331 Architecture Building
Gainesville, FL 32611
www.arch.ufl.edu/landscape/index.html

University of Georgia (B.L.A., M.L.A.)
Program in Landscape Architecture
School of Environmental Design
609 Caldwell Hall
Athens, GA 30602-1845
www.cyclops.sed.uga.edu

University of Idaho (B.L.A.)
Landscape Architecture Department
College of Art and Architecture
Moscow, ID 83844-2481
www.uidaho.edu/larch

University of Illinois (B.L.A., M.L.A.)
Department of Landscape Architecture
College of Fine and Applied Arts
101 Buell Hall MC 620, 611 Taft Drive
Champaign, IL 61820
www.uiuc.edu/admin_manual/PoS/majors/LA.html

University of Kentucky (B.S.L.A.)
Department of Landscape Architecture
N318 Agriculture Science North
Lexington, KY 40546-0091
www.uky.edu/Agriculture/LA

University of Maryland (B.L.A.)
Landscape Architecture Program
Department of Natural Resource Sciences and Landscape Architecture
2146 Plant Sciences Building
College Park, MD 20742
www.larch.umd.edu

University of Massachusetts (B.S.L.A., M.L.A.)
Department of Landscape Architecture and Regional Planning
Hills North 109
Amherst, MA 01003
www-unix.oit.umass.edu/~larp

University of Michigan (M.L.A.)
Landscape Architecture
School of Natural Resources and Environment
Dana Building, 430 East University
Ann Arbor, MI 48109-1115
www.snre.umich.edu/la

University of Minnesota (M.L.A.)
Department of Landscape Architecture
1425 University Avenue SE, Room 115
Minneapolis, Minnesota 55414

University of Nevada, Las Vegas (B.L.A.)
School of Architecture, Sogg Architecture Building
4505 Maryland Parkway
Las Vegas, NV 89154-4018
www.unlv.edu/Colleges/Fine_Arts/Architecture/laarch/LAlandscape.htm

University of Oklahoma (M.L.A.—Provisional)
Landscape Architecture Program
Gould Hall, Room 162
Norman, OK 73019-0265
www.uoknor.edu/architecture/dla/idland.htm

University of Oregon (B.L.A.)
Department of Landscape Architecture
School of Architecture and Allied Arts
Eugene, OR 97403-5234
www.lazarus.uoregon.edu/~landar/LAdept.html

University of Pennsylvania (M.L.A.)
Department of Landscape Architecture and Regional Planning
Graduate School of Fine Arts
119 Myerson Hall, 210 South Thirty-Fourth Street
Philadelphia, PA 19104-6311
www.dolphin.upenn.edu/~gsfa/larp/index.html

University of Rhode Island (B.L.A.)
Landscape Architecture Program
6 Greenhouse Road, Room 207
Kingston, RI 02881
www.uri.edu/cels/lar

University of Texas—Arlington (M.L.A.)
P.O. Box 19108
Arlington, TX 76019-0108

University of Virginia (M.L.A.)
Department of Landscape Architecture
School of Architecture
Campbell Hall
Charlottesville, VA 22903
www.minerva.acc.Virginia.EDU/~arch

University of Washington (B.L.A., M.L.A.)
Department of Landscape Architecture
College of Architecture and Urban Planning
348 Gould Hall, Box 355734
Seattle, WA 98195-5734
www.caup.washington.edu/HTML/LARCH

University of Wisconsin (B.S.L.A.)
Department of Landscape Architecture
School of Natural Resources
College of Agricultural and Life Sciences
Room 1, Agriculture Hall
1450 Linden Drive
Madison, WI 53706

Utah State University (B.L.A., M.L.A.)
Department of Landscape Architecture and Environmental Planning
College of Humanities, Arts and Social Sciences
Logan, UT 84322-4005

Virginia Polytechnic Institute and State University (B.L.A., M.L.A.)
Landscape Architecture Department
College of Architecture and Urban Studies
202 Architecture Annex
Blacksburg, VA 24061-0113
www.lar.arch.vt.edu

Washington State University (B.L.A.)
Department of Horticulture and Landscape Architecture
College of Agriculture and Home Economics
Johnson Hall 149
Pullman, WA 99164-6414
www.coopext.cahe.wsu.edu/~hortla

West Virginia University (B.S.L.A.— Provisional)
Chair of the Landscape Architecture Program
College of Agriculture and Forestry
1142 Agricultural Sciences Building
Morgantown, WV 26506-6108
www.caf.wvu.edu/resm/la/index.html

Canada

The following programs are accredited by the Canadian Society of Landscape
Architects Accreditation Council:

University of British Columbia (M.L.A.)
Landscape Architecture Program
6368 Stores Road
Vancouver, BC V6T 1Z4

University of Guelph (B.L.A., M.L.A.)
School of Landscape Architecture
University of Guelph
Guelph, Ontario, N1G 2W1
www.uoguelph.ca/Landscape_Architecture

University of Manitoba (M.L.A.)
Department of Landscape Architecture
Room 220, Architecture II
Winnipeg, MB R3T 2N2

Université de Montréal
BLA Program
École d'archtecture de paysage
5620 Avenue Darlington, #3019
C.P. 6128, Succursale A
Montréal, QC H3C 3J7
www.apa.umontreal.ca

University of Toronto (B.L.A. currently being phased out, M.L.A under
   review)
Programme in Landscape Architecture
Faculty of Architecture, Landscape, and Design
230 College Street
Toronto, ON M5T 1R2
www.clr.utoronto.ca